Yoginī

Yoginī
The Shady Side of Devī

Guido Zanderigo

Translated from Italian by
Christine Harris

DK PRINTWORLD
Publishers of Indian Traditions

Cataloging in Publication Data – DK
[Courtesy: D.K. Agencies (P) Ltd. <docinfo@dkagencies.com>]

Zanderigo, Guido, author.
Yoginī : the shady side of Devī / Guido Zanderigo ; translated from Italian by Christine Harris.
pages cm
Includes bibliographical references and index.
ISBN 9788124608463

1. Yoginīs. 2. Yoginīs — Cult. 3. Tantrism. I. Harris, Christine (Translator), translator. II. Title.

BL1216.2.Z36 2015 DDC 294.52114 23

ISBN 978-81-246-0846-3
First published in Italian in 2012
English translation first published in India in 2016

Printed and published by:
D.K. Printworld (P) Ltd.
Regd. Office: *Vedaśrī*, F-395, Sudarshan Park
(Metro Station: Ramesh Nagar), New Delhi – 110 015
Phones: (011) 2545 3975, 2546 6019; *Fax*: (011) 2546 5926
e-mail: indology@dkprintworld.com
Website: www.dkprintworld.com

Preface

THE text awaiting the reader in the following pages is the fruit of a long study, wide reading and, above all, of the three the Venetian Acadmey of Indian Studies (VAIS) missions to Assam and Arunachal Pradesh. Little known and even less visited by scholars of Indian culture, these two states of the Indian Union, surrounded by the southern foothills of the easternmost part of the Himalayan chain and the banks of the vast Brahmaputra, are characterized by a massive presence of Tantric and Śākta schools rooted in a sacred geography which is evidently allusive, but tricky to interpret. Here traditional culture is well preserved, but somewhat turned in on itself, in a kind of isolation not deliberately defensive, but which jealously protects its mysterious traditions. It is even more difficult to penetrate the reserve of the numerous initiatory schools (*saṁpradāyas*) whose rigorously esoteric nature impedes any approach by the profane investigator.

Thanks to credentials obtained from some of the highest spiritual authorities in Benares, Guido Zanderigo was able to set out to conquer this world, taking the temple of Kāmākhyā itself as a point of departure to enter the mythical kingdom of Kāmarūpa. It was a journey full of surprises, since the investigation touched on very different areas, and required research and verification in the fields of philology and textual analysis, iconography, mythology, astronomy, ethnology and comparative cultural studies, to name only the more academic aspects, all of which the author managed with ease.

However, the most delicate task was a patient cutting and stitching of more subtle kinds of knowledge, which required methodological competence, reflection on techniques of invocation and on iconographic and yantric supports for meditation, along with a clear evaluation of elements having to do with inner states, visions, mantric vibrations, and the acquisition of no-ordinary states of consciousness — all domains which elude profane scientific research. To this was added the task of putting in order a tangle of traditions which is usually classified as belonging either to "cultured" Hinduism or to the folklore of the peasant masses, or to that form of Buddhism which is wrongly considered to be corrupt and "magical", or to the so-called tribal religions.

In the end all the tiles of the mosaic fitted into the right places, and the resulting picture appears homogeneous, with content of a high level: Dr Zanderigo has managed to describe the esoteric cult of the sixty-four Yoginīs by connecting it with other great initiatory traditions of Tantrism, particularly with the Śrīvidyā, the most intellectual of the Śākta schools. Since time immemorial, this last school of thought has always been closely entwined with the lineage of masters of Advaita Vedānta; it remains very much alive today, following the teachings of the *Tripurārahasya Upaniṣad*. Mysteriously, this Śākta school of the right-hand path is practically ignored by Indologists, Western and otherwise, who prefer to study defunct Tantric schools with no living authorities, thereby avoiding the embarrassment of being contradicted.

The author's task was not easy, but the results delivered in this book are of a very high level. The Yoginīs are described here in all their multiple facets, while always maintaining a fundamental unity. The few scholars who have gone so far as to tackle this subject in the recent past have tended to distinguish the Yoginīs into diverse categories: according to them the Yoginīs were sometimes deities, sometimes women devoted to the black arts, or witches, sometimes demons or ghostly apparitions, sometimes tribal intrusions into the superstitions of the lowest levels of the Hindu society.

The novelty of this study consists in its demonstration of the underlying unity of this esoteric cult, starting from the evidence that the Yoginīs, regardless of which of their many aspects they show, are always iconographically represented in the same way. And as Dr Zanderigo explains, this underlying unity is due to the fact that they are none other than the different powers of the one Goddess who makes the world manifest, powers which must always be regarded from a viewpoint of self-realization, outside any schematic framework or compilation.

This is quite unlike, for example, R.K. Sharma in his *The Temple of Chaunsatha-yogini at Bheraghat*, which certainly deals competently with the iconography and history of the Yoginīs, but dares not to offer any hypothesis which might explain the importance of their cult in Tantric initiatory circles, maintaining a purely descriptive approach devoid of critical analysis. Nor does D.G. White, in his recent book *Kiss of the Yogini: 'Tantric Sex' in Its South Asian Contexts*, despite great erudition, take us even one step further towards an understanding of their mystery, entirely absorbed as he is by the prurient implications of the indecent Freudianism in vogue in the Chicago school of Indology, further enriched by a New Age inclination towards the search for powers (*siddhi*).

Only Vidya Dehejia, in her *Yogini Cult and Temples: A Tantric Tradition*, has come anywhere near the correct method for solving the mystery of the Yoginī. This scholar worked in the right direction, with ample references to religious practice and explorations of the texts. What Dehejia foresaw, but without bringing the task to completion, is precisely the methodical pursuit of self-realization which the symbolism of the Yoginī implies. And this concludes our review of those who have studied this theme.

From this point of view the present book appears substantially complete, and further allows us a wide range of comparisons with other complementary female figures who stand beside or stand in for the Yoginīs. I refer above all to the Saptamātr̥kā and to the ten Mahāvidyās, whose functions and attributes can be discovered in the following pages. Along with these, the author considers the Ḍākinī and the Nityā — functions in a feminine key which are common to the Hindu and Buddhist traditions. The third cultural component which Dr Zanderigo always bears in mind is the so-called tribal element, which he invokes whenever the theme of the Yoginīs is entwined with phenomena of shamanic or oracular possession. This last domain is of great importance as an archive of information about Indian traditions, yet there is a serious shortage of academic studies about it. The plurimillennial contact between Brāhmanic Hinduism and other currents of Hinduism has led to the formation of a compact whole which is impossible to unravel. For that matter, the *vanajāti*, far from being tribes in the literal sense of cultural anthropology, are in reality simply forest castes.[1] And, we would add, in almost all the Tantric temples in India, oracular rites officiated by tribal groups are quite at home.

This book is also furnished with a great number of images, selected as didactic illustrations of the lines of argument unfolding from chapter to chapter, which are extremely useful for the profound understanding of a text which at a conceptual level is not always within everybody's reach. Furthermore, the entire book is written in elegant, fluent and colourful prose, which keeps the subject matter so rich in implications and free of the pedantry of academic exposition.

Gian Giuseppe Filippi

---

1 *Ādivāsī*, the Ghandian term used for tribal people, is not only imprecise, but has also had the effect of separating tribals from other Hindus. Until the nineteenth century marriages with tribal people were commonplace even at princely level. But ever since the tribals were distinguished from other Indians, first by the British, then by independent India, such marriages have ceased.

Contents

List of Plates

Note

I thank the following institutions for giving permission to publish their images in this book:

www.ethnos.biz by Ethnica
www.exoticindia.com
www.wikipedia.org
www.common.wikimedia.org

It was not possible to trace owners of images in some cases. Please inform me at <zanderigog@gmail.com> for ownership of any photograph so that the same may be credited to him/her in future edition.

Introduction

Thus She is the ultimate, unified Śakti,
the Parameśvarī,
triple Tripurā,
the very self of Brahmā, Viṣṇu and Īśa;
the Being who is Jñāna-Śakti, Kriyā-Śakti and Icchā-Śakti
— *Vāmakeśvarīmatam* IV.10-11

INDIA has always revealed herself through an excess of signs.

Her cosmogonies hang in clusters from the One, each of them juicy with water and blood. Her epics are oceanic, all-pervading, tentacular. Her myths invariably labyrinthine, not so much in their basic plots as in the way their outlines fade into digressions which become entangled, mixing up the characters, playing havoc with landmarks, realigning the boundaries between light and darkness. We have learned to move warily through these stratifications, always ready for a sudden swerve.

And yet nothing had prepared us for the unfathomable depths of the Yoginīs. Even at first glance, something about them escapes us. What is their nature? What are they made of? Where do they belong in the precise geometries of the cosmos? Yoginīs elude these categories, confusing the manifester with what is made manifest, knowledge with what is known. So their game seems to play out elsewhere, in an inclination towards the mysterious and nocturnal, in that half light where those who cannot see take a rope to be a snake.

Endowed with a thousand faces, dripping with blood, Yoginīs lurk on the sidelines, waiting with the patience of those who know that you must eventually take this path — crouching behind a tree at the *tīrtha,* just below the surface of its pool, or hidden in the earth of the burial mound. They do not dispense the blandishments of kindly gods. The Yoginīs tear, strip, eviscerate; and they do it without offering relief, without the compromise of pity.

Instinctively, almost all of us try to escape their clutches. Only the best of us run towards that embrace with an inebriated smile. And yet we will meet them in the end, one way or another. Because the Yoginīs keep company with death, whether it comes as a reunion with the Absolute or as our personal surrender.

1

The Nature of the Yoginīs

In practice, in the Indian tradition the term *yoginī* designates different categories of female beings who all appear as genuine expressions of the divine, whether in subtle form or in simple human guise.

This diversification is also found in the sphere of Vajrayāna Buddhism, where Yoginīs are assimilated with Ḍākinī (Tibetan *Khandroma*) — literally "those who fly in the sky" — subdivided into secret Ḍākinī (Tibetan *yum chenmo*), reflections of transcendent wisdom (*Prajñāpāramitā*), inner Ḍākinī (Vajraḍākinī), who act as spiritual guides (Tibetan *yidam*) during meditation, outer Ḍākinī, who act on the practitioner's subtle body, and completely external Ḍākinī found in human form as women dedicated to *yoga* or as consorts of *yogin*s with great powers (*mahāsiddha*).

Even in this variety of aspects, *yoginī*s seem to maintain a few common characteristics, such as their association with fierce animals, especially beasts and birds of prey, their links with possession and sacrifice, their development of powers, including flight, and a nocturnal quality which alludes to their mastery over those interstices in the cyclic maelstrom of time which harbour the promise and the terror of annihilation. Above all, a character of secrecy along with a disquieting, even sinister, reputation has allowed them to remain "under the radar", remote from any too explicit popular devotion, as an unequivocal passage in *Kaulajñāna Nirṇaya*[1] sets out:

> The Yoginīs received the wisdom which yoga manifests instantaneously. This wisdom was called Yoginī Kaula[2] because it never went beyond the limits of their circle.

Although they are found all over India, these typically Tantric elements seem to assume particular importance in the sacred geography of Assam, unfolding in myths and allusions in the name of subtle knowledge and its protean manifestations in female form — such as *devī, mahāvidyā, mātṛkā, grāmadevatā, bālagraha* or *yakṣiṇī* — all bent on redefining the paths to redemption amid bloody rites, mystic seductions and *danses macabres*.

---

1 *Kaulajñāna Nirṇaya,* a ninth-century Tantric text containing ritual and magic formulae, is a cornerstone of both Hindu and Vajrayāna Buddhist Tantric schools. It is attributed to Matsyendranātha, the *siddha* who was a point of reference for the school of the Kānphaṭa *yogī,* a school which constitutes a watershed between original Tantrism and its medieval developments. Matsyendranātha describes himself as the founder of the Yoginī Kaula tradition, a doctrine which reformed the earlier Siddha Kaula schools of Kashmir and gave rise to the so-called Eastern tradition which took root in Kāmarūpa (Assam). He is regarded as the superhuman intermediary who "brought down the original Tantric revelation to the lunar site of Candra-dvīpa (the continent of the moon) or Candra-giri (the hill of the moon)". The separation in time between those who proclaim themselves his direct disciples suggests that Matsyendranātha is a function rather than a real historical person.

For more details, see David Gordon White, *The Alchemical Body,* 1996.

2 *Kaula* means those of the *kula* family, the family of Kālī, and was the name assumed by a Tantric school which developed in north-eastern India between Bengal and Assam. The secrecy of the "family's" doctrines and rituals is confirmed in *Śrīmātottara Tantra,* each chapter of which ends with a warning that the material dealt with is *yoginī guhya* (a secret of the Yoginī). — Dehejia 1986.

2

Yoginīs as Deities

THE most exalted aspect of the Yoginīs places them in direct relation to the Devī, so that among her epithets we find Yoginī or Yoganirata (she who practises *yoga*), Yogamaya (she whose substance is *yoga*) and Yogānandapradāyinī (she who grants bliss through *yoga*). This is made even more explicit in *Viṣṇubhāgavata Purāṇa,* in which the Goddess is called Mahāyoginī (the great Yoginī), while in *Lalitā Sahasranāma*[1] She is Kula Yoginī, the Yoginī assimilated with Kālī. And among the Thousand Names of the Devī, the officiant may invoke Her with the words "You are Yoginī".

This interchangeability of names and functions is a clear sign of how, in the maze of streams which flowed into the Śākta tradition, there remains an overlapping between the Goddess, unique and primordial — hence an aspect of the supreme Deity, from this doctrinal perspective — and the forms through which she manifests; so that many Hindu and Buddhist sources in one way or another identify Devī (the Goddess) with Śakti (feminine expression-power of the divine), Yoginī and Ḍākinī.

Moving from the sphere of the sole Devī to her capacity to subdivide and replicate herself in garlands of names, facets or subordinate aspects, we meet the Yoginī in ranks of diverse

---

[1] *Lalitā Sahasranāma* is one of the most sacred texts of devotion to the Goddess; it enumerates her thousand names in the form of a hymn whose recitation leads to the ultimate liberation. The hymn is found in the *Brahmāṇḍa Purāṇa* as a dialogue between Hayagrīva and the sage Agastya.

number — 16, 42, 50 or 81 — although most commonly they gather in groups of 64.

According to *Caṇḍī Purāṇa*,[2] in fact, they were formed from sixty-four parts of the body of the Goddess and represent the darkest Ḍākinī, the bringers of death. A similar vision recurs in the Aruṇācala Māhātmya section of *Skanda Purāṇa*, according to which the Goddess created the circle of sixty-four Yoginīs (Cauṅsaṭha-Yoginī) from her own body to fight the demon Mahiṣāsura. And it is precisely in a circle of Yoginīs that *Pheṭkāriṇī Tantra*[3] prescribes that she must be adored in her form as Śmaśānakālikā, the Goddess Kālī of the cemeteries.

Already in these first few allusions, assembling in a circle (*cakra* or *maṇḍala*) emerges as a distinctive characteristic of Yoginī, recalling those magic circles which populated the woods of the West with fantastic female creatures. This characteristic recurs in the atypically circular plan of their temples (*fig*. 1), where the Cauṅsatha-Yoginī form a ring facing inwards on the empty courtyard, almost as if they had cut a clearing out of the tangle of the jungle. These places of worship are invariably secluded, hidden in the depths of the forest or crowning isolated hilltops: sylvan assemblies of Yoginīs fixed in stone either by time or by some arcane magic, at the centre of which the presence of the God Bhairava, dancing naked, evokes the unbridled power of

---

[2] *Caṇḍī Purāṇa*, a text composed in Orissa in the fifteenth century by Śūdramuni Sāralā Dās, returns to the myth of Durgā's killing of the demon Mahiṣāsura. The story tells how the Goddess Caṇḍī generated sixty-four Yoginīs avid for blood, bone and marrow, who are always ready to fight demons and feed on them.

[3] *Pheṭkāriṇī Tantra*, along with *Nīla Tantra*, is indicated by Śiva as a means for obtaining power (Śakti), knowledge (Sarasvatī) and wealth (Lakṣmī). It is one of the darkest texts of the left-hand path, and confers the power to control the Devī in her jackal form using particularly sinister ritual supports like the *pheṭkāriṇī mālā*, a rosary made from the bones of a woman who died in childbirth.

the Bacchantes. These temples are doubly anomalous because within their low perimeter walls there is no *garbhagṛha* (altar for sacred oblations), a womb usually embedded in the mass of Hindu temples whose chimney serves to convey the smoke from burnt offerings towards the sky. But since sacrifice remains the foundation of any ritual it must take place nevertheless, taking on a different and much crueller nature.

The sculptures of Yoginīs lining the perimeter wall (*fig*. 2) often present a female body with the head of an animal (*fig*. 3), alluding to tendencies shared with that creature or to the power to subjugate it and absorb its characteristics (strength, capacity to fly, claws and fangs ready to dismember, poisonous bite, etc.). And it is no accident that the very mounts (*vāhanas*) on which they are seated — a varied bestiary which includes owls, vultures, jackals, elephants, horses, wild beasts and snakes — correspond to the animals which, in *Kaulajñāna Nirṇaya,* Śiva describes as forms assumed by Yoginī in order to move across the earth, thus anticipating the theme of possession-substitution which we will find again in tribal contexts as a key element of shamanic trance. One kind of movement which remains typical of the Yoginīs is flight, either using *vetāla, preta,* corpses or skulls as celestial steeds for their aerial forays or else, as the *Dvyāśraya* suggests, by being directly assimilated with menacing birds of the night.[4]

However, the traditional lists of Yoginīs (*nāmāvalī*) do not keep to a single unequivocal compilation, differing considerably one from another and showing strong local characteristics.

---

4 Similarly, Yoginī can be depicted with human bodies and birds' heads, as in the case of Jauti, of Umā or of Piṅgalā, one of the sixty-four Yoginīs of the temple of Bherāghāṭ. The same elements recur in Śakunī, one of the *mātṛkā-bālagrahas*, who is described in *Suśruta Saṁhitā* and in *Harivaṁśa Purāṇa* as a bird which flies through the sky roaring like a tiger, or in *Mahābhārata* as a *pakṣiṇī* (female bird) which moves in the blackness of night — White, 2003.

In these lists one often encounters the names of the *mātṛkās* (mothers), deities found all over India who act as a link between popular projections of the forces of nature and aspects of feminine power of the major hypostases of Hindu gods.

In *Agni Purāṇa* and *Devī Māhātmya*[5] Yoginīs are associated with the Aṣṭamātṛkā (eight principal forms of the Devī, from whom derive the sixty-four Yoginīs in groups of eight.

The Aṣṭamātṛkā constitute an extension of the more classic group of seven mothers (Saptamātṛkā) — Brāhmī, Māheśvarī, Aindrī-Indrāṇī, Kaumārī, Vaiṣṇavī, Vārāhī and Cāmuṇḍā — who are habitually accompanied by Mahālakṣmī or Yogeśvarī (*Varāha Purāṇa*), that same Yogeśvarī who is considered a Yoginī, which further reinforces the relationship between Mātṛkās and Yoginīs.

The myths about the origins of the Mātṛkās which are narrated in the Purāṇa have in common the theme of the bloody struggle between the gods — Śiva, Viṣṇu or Indra, depending on the source — and the demon Andhakāsura (elsewhere replaced by Raktabija), whose blood continuously regenerates new demons as it drips on to the ground (*fig*. 4a, b). So the Mātṛkās are created to drink this blood as soon as it gushes from his wounds, thereby preventing multiplication of the *asura.* The tale encloses an evident symbolic meaning since the Mātṛkā-Yoginīs, by stopping the dripping of blood and hence drying up the source of regeneration, reduce multiplicity to unity — an essential condition for the cessation of the flow of *māyā* with its illusory production of forms. And it is precisely this sacrifice of the *asura* which is the instrument that overcomes contingency

---

5 *Devī Māhātmya* or *Caṇḍī Pāṭha,* which is considered the most important work of reference by Śākta schools, was composed around the fifth century CE and makes up the 74th to 86th chapters of *Mārkaṇḍeya Purāṇa.* It consists of 700 (*saptaśata*) verses and for this reason is also called *Durgā Saptaśatī.* Once again, the narrative centres on Durgā's battle against the demon Mahiṣāsura.

and guarantees reintegration into primordial unity.

Varāha Purāṇa, however, offers a significant variant, relating the Aṣṭamātṛkā to the eight diabolical qualities of Andhakāsura in that, once their terrible task has been completed and they have absorbed the qualities of the demon through his blood, their savage nature must be controlled by *vidyā* (sacred knowledge). In this guise Yogeśvarī comes to embody *kāma* (desire), Māheśvarī *krodha* (anger), Vaiṣṇavī *lobha* (avidity), Brahmāṇī *mada* (pride), Kaumārī *moha* (illusion), Indrāṇī *mātsarya* (sin), Yamī or Cāmuṇḍā *paiśuṇya* (falsity) and Vārāhī *asūyā* (envy). It follows that the āsuric forces — first cause of manifestation — and the tremendous consequences they unleash can only be governed by knowledge, which is none other than a doctrinal transposition of what sacrifice represents in ritual terms.

On the other hand, the overlapping between the Mātṛkās and diabolical elements introduces one of the central and perhaps most contradictory characteristics of the Indian world of gods, at least from the Western viewpoint in which good and evil are polar opposites: the Goddess tends to appear and act according to a dual nature, presenting herself to the faithful as a benevolent mother, a protector and saviour, and at the same time as an irate and ravenous, unfathomable dispenser of illness and death. *Vidyā* (sacred knowledge) is therefore the key to circumscribing and bringing under control the power latent in this dark side, a power which is in any case necessary if one is to undertake the process of individual transformation.

It is precisely the dark side which is emphasized in much of the literature regarding the Yoginīs, emerging as a salient feature of their way of manifesting.

In the eighth *paṭala* of *Yoginī Tantra*,[6] Śiva describes them as

---

[6] *Yoginī Tantra*, a sixteenth-century text from Assam, is one of the works of reference for the Vāmācāra tradition (otherwise known as the "left-hand path"), which follows the more extreme Tantric practices.

dreadful creatures with innumerable faces and flaming eyes.

Yaśastilaka[7] relates how the Mahāyoginīs, attendants of Caṇḍamāri, appeared in the sky at nightfall, rushing across the vault of heaven so impetuously that their plaited hair loosened and streamed out behind them.[8] Their cheeks were daubed with designs in blood; during their flight their necklaces, bracelets and anklets jingled furiously, while fragments broke off the skullcaps they clutched in their hands. After sticking their tongues out between their sharp fangs to drink of the waters of the celestial Gaṅgā, thereby arousing the disapproval of the *saptarṣi* — the constellation of the Bear or, in symbolic terms, the repository of knowledge of the Veda — the Mahāyoginīs resumed their descent, darkening the sky with their long-flowing hair and sending sinister flashes of light from the skulls set in their crowns, which shone like stars in the blackness of night.[9]

A tremendous force emerges from this grim but fascinating description, a vibration of power which shakes the cosmos in

---

7 A Jaina text of the Śaka period composed by Somadeva Sūri in CE 881 or, according to other sources, in CE 939. This account is taken from Dehejia 1986.

8 The loosening of plaits traditionally indicates the menstrual period and is therefore a sign of the "menstruating" nature of the Goddess. A significant comparison can be made with the passage in *Mahābhārata* in which Draupadī loosens her plaits and soaks them in the blood of Duḥśāsana in the battle of Kurukṣetra between Pāṇḍavas and Kauravas (Giovanni Torcinovich and Gian Giuseppe Filippi, *Draupadī: il culto femminile e il ciclo della Dea madre*, VAIS lecture at the Società Letteraria of Verona, 7 May 2004).

9 In cosmological terms the celestial Gaṅgā corresponds to the Milky Way. This equivalence is found again in the fragments broken from the skull-caps (*kapāla*) and strewn throughout the skies by the Mahāyoginīs, symbolically recalling the crushed and ground bones of the dead which formed the star dust of the Milky Way. — Santillana and von Dechend 1969.

the primordial night. And on the other hand, loosened plaits of hair streaming in all directions evoke Śiva Naṭarāja's hair during the dance of cosmic creation and destruction, symbolic of the divine mysteries which measure out the universe, penetrating all of its components.[10]

The association of the Goddess with nocturnal darkness is found again in *Devī-Māhātmya*, where her epithets are Mahā-māyā (Great Illusion), Kāla-rātri (Black Night of Time), Mahā-rātri (Great Night) and Moha-rātri (Deceptive Night).

This viewpoint is taken up in the Tantric sphere by the Daśamahāvidyā (literally "the ten great sciences"), esoteric expressions of the Devī related to Śākta Tantrism which serve mainly as supports in spiritual practice (*sādhanā*) rather than mere objects of devotion (*bhakti*).[11] But apart from necessary distinctions between the features and functions of a single *mahāvidyā*, there are constant references to their nocturnal nature, so much so that each one is identified with a specific type of night.[12]

This confirms of what has so far emerged about the nature of the Devī, where night becomes a precise reference to a temporal setting, or rather to a concurrence of conditions, over which she exercises her tremendous dominion between one cycle of manifestation and the next. Night becomes a metaphor for a suspension of illusory reality during which the Goddess opens her maw, offering the adept capable of seeing beyond appearances an escape route from the flow of multiplicity, from that illusion (*māyā*), which is nothing less than one of her thousand names.

One of the murkiest instances of this character of the *mahāvidyā* is Dhūmāvatī (the smoky Goddess), known also by

---

10 Filippi 1978c.

11 Ramasso 2010.

12 Daniélou 1964.

the name of Dhūmravārāhī[13] — who, according to *Tantrarāja*,[14] incarnates the principle of non-existence, black night (Kāla-rātri), great night of death and dissolution, pitiless night (Dāruṇa-rātri) in which all is lost. She is the divine mother at the time of the flood, when the world lay below the waters; she evokes that tremendous emptiness following the final apocalypse (*pralaya*) which at the same time precedes the creation.

The solitude which permeates Dhūmāvatī makes her the only *mahāvidyā* without a masculine counterpart, which is why she is called Vidhavā (widow). Her iconographic attributes include all the elements tending to instil revulsion and terror: two long fangs, blood all over her body and clothes, withered

---

13 Dhūmrāvārāhī appears as one of the names of Mahāvārāhī among the twenty-seven secret (*rahasya*) names of *Śrīvidyā Āmnāyakrama*, along with Vāsya-Vārāhī, Astra-Vārāhī, Bṛhad-Vārāhī, Kirāta-Vārāhī and Strustambhana-Vartalī, all connected with the direction south. In the light of what follows, the name Kirāta-Vārāhī seems particularly significant, because the Kirātas are a mountain people devoted to the ritual consumption of meat and wine linked with the cult of Kāmākhyā.

14 *Tantrarāja Tantra*, or king of Tantras, deals with the three forms (*rūpa*s) of the Goddess Tripurasundarī: the supreme, the subtle and the gross, and the consequent forms of her cult involving mind, speech and body. The text is traditionally numbered among the sixty-four principal Tantra texts composed between the sixth and fifteenth centuries on the basis of pre-existing cults and practices. They are grouped according to the deity they refer to, so that the twenty-eight classic Āgamas (*mūlāgama*s) are considered Tantra of the Śaiva area, while the *Pāñcarātra* and the *Vaikhānasa* are considered Vaiṣṇava, and those ascribed to the Śākta area — or true Tantra — are *Mahānirvāṇa*, *Kulārṇava*, *Prapañcasāra*, *Tantrarāja*, *Rudrayāmala*, *Brahmayāmala*, *Viṣṇuyāmala* and *Toḍala*. The Tantra also spread to Jaina and Buddhist circles, so that a Mahāyāna *Tantrarāja Tantra* exists — its full name is *Paramādibuddhoddhṛta Śrī Kālacakra nāme Tantrarāja* — which is linked with the doctrine of *kālacakra* (the wheel of time).

breasts, corpses and chopped-off hands worn as earrings and a *muṇḍamālā* (string of skulls or severed heads) for a necklace (*fig.* 5). The black raven on her standard, a symbol of dark forces, completes this sinister picture — that same raven which is found again in the title of a Tantric text of the left-hand path, the Kākacaṇḍeśvarīmata (the point of view of the terrible Lady [with the face of a] raven).[15]

The meditative practice (*upāsanā*) dedicated to Dhūmāvatī is carried out on the dark nights of the new moon[16] in some solitary place — a forest or cemetery — where the naked *sādhaka* sits facing south. It is a power ritual which makes it possible to reach trance and *samādhi* through the ten cosmic powers identified with the Daśamahāvidyā themselves.

This proximity to the phenomenon of trance is confirmed by the winnowing fan (*śūrpa*) that She holds in her hand, making it a symbol of the separation (or sifting) of the perishable physical body from that which lasts beyond death, and at the same time an instrument whose rhythmic shaking allows the shaman to reach the state of trance.[17] But unlike shamanic phenomena

---

15 References to the funereal character of ravens are already found in the Vedic tradition, which attests that the souls of the dead appear to their relatives in the form of ravens, thus becoming identified with Maruts, to act as psychopomps during the cremation rite. — Filippi 1999.

16 The night of the new moon is called *amāvasyā* (union), in Sanskrit because it is the time when the moon (*soma*) and sun (*agni*) are closest to each other. It is then that mimed sexual union between the queen and the horse sacrificed in the course of the Aśvamedha takes place, symbolizing union with the king and the oblation of seminal fluid in the fire of the female matrix. — Arnoldo 2002.

17 The winnowing fan (*śūrpa*) is a wide tray made of plaited fibres used in India and South-East Asia to bounce grains of rice or wheat up into the air so that the wind separates them from the chaff, which it blows away. The sound of the grains falling rhythmically back on to the winnowing fan is used to accompany the dance of the shaman, →

connected with access to some intermediate world, the purpose of trance here is the attainment of powers (*siddhi*) to open the path to ultimate knowledge.

These are characteristics which, going back in time, can be traced to the Vedic Nirr̥ti (*fig.* 6), black night, the goddess who is the mother of Mr̥tyu (Death), a tenebrous deity who in *Atharvaveda* personifies bad luck, decadence and destruction, and in *R̥gveda* sickness and dissolution. In the post-Vedic period she turns into Nirr̥ta, the *dikpāla* who is the guardian of the south — a direction which indeed is connected with death.

Her terrifying nature is confirmed in *Mānava Dharmaśāstra* (*The Book of the Law of Manu*), which suggests that her anger be placated through the nocturnal sacrifice of a cross-eyed ass at a crossroads. The ass is an allusion to dark forces and along with the winnowing fan, it is found again in representations of Śītalā, Goddess of smallpox.[18]

And yet, in the inevitable and necessary inversion of perspective typical of the Hindu world-view, just like death, Nirr̥ti herself must also be killed. And it was to carry out this task that Brahmā generated the Saptamātr̥kā, according to a variant of their myth found in *Suprabhedāgama*. Here however the killing seems to imply less an overcoming than a substitution, in which the Mātr̥kās end up taking on some of the characteristics of Nirr̥ti–Dhūmāvatī, also in their iconography. This emerges clearly in Cāmuṇḍā who, like Dūmāvatī, is the only one without a male counterpart because she was generated by the very fury of the Goddess. This peculiarity is borne out in the earliest sculptures of the Saptamātr̥kā, where she is the only one in the group to be depicted with four arms, confirming her divine autonomy.

←   which — faster and faster — brings him to a state of trance. For further details, see Filippi 2002.

[18]   Filippi 2002.

So Cāmuṇḍā is the terrible aspect of the supreme Devī who unleashes the latent power of nature (*prakṛti*), a fury consecrated to battle and destruction. She is Kālī who defeats and beheads the demons Caṇḍa and Muṇḍa (from whom she gets her name). She is one of the Mātṛkās who dance, drunk with blood, at the end of Durgā's battle with the demons Śumbha and Niśumbha.[19]

We are in the presence of a terrifying hypostasis, a power whose howl is like that of a hundred jackals, worthy attendants often depicted at her feet lapping up blood from *kapāla* and severed heads. But they are not the only horrible companions encircling her, because among the innumerable variants of her iconography, Cāmuṇḍā's extended entourage may include *piśāca* (doleful spirits often originating from the lack of a proper funeral ceremony), *preta* (spirits of the dead), *bhūta* (spectres caused by the decomposition of corpses), cadavers, lions, leopards, hyenas and owls (*fig*. 7). The noose which holds them in thrall (*pāśa*) is her sign. A tigerskin encircles her hips. And to placate her, one does not hesitate to offer wine and sacrifices in her name, sacrifices which originally were human undoubtedly.

Finally, she is invoked to pacify the *bālagraha*, entities which dispense illness to children — a further proof of her sinister power over life and death.

But if Cāmuṇḍā is characterized by a terrifying appearance and the lack of a fixed canon, Vārāhī also stands out from the group of Saptamātṛkās, giving rise to a variety of portrayals and prompting noteworthy interpretations, starting from her aspect as the wild boar goddess — that is, she who digs with her tusks to bring to light what is hidden under the surface or has been lost, suggesting a kind of luminous counterpart to the darkness of Cāmuṇḍā (*fig*. 8).

---

19 Marchetto 2002. In the Mahiṣamardinī-Stotra of *Devī-Māhātmya*, the theme of plaited hair recurs when Devī, in the terrible form of Durgā, is described with "her long plaited hair like a mass of clouds covering her terrifying face".

To obtain specific favours, *Tantrarāja Tantra* prescribes that Vārāhī must be visualized on the back of a lion (like Durgā when she kills the buffalo Mahiṣa), a tiger, an elephant, a horse or an eagle (*garuḍa*), all animals implying action against the to forces of darkness.

Varāhī is also considered to be a real Yoginī with a boar's head, an assimilation confirmed in the Vajrayāna sphere where, among the deities cited in *Anuttarayoga Tantra*,[20] we find Yoginī-Vārāhī along with Yamāri (she who opposes Yama, or Death), Yamāntaka (destroyer of Death) and Tārā.

And yet these characteristics do not hinder a kind of contiguity between Vārāhī and death, as if her function must be enacted through it rather than outside it. Like Yama, she is accompanied by a buffalo and she drinks blood from a *kapāla*, which associates her with the destructive energy of the God of the underworld. Moreover, the *Śilpa-Saṁgraha* describes Vārāhī as the daughter of Yama, while Hemādri[21] affirms that she is Yamī, twin sister of the God of Death. And then Vārāhī is regarded as a *rātrī-devatā* (nocturnal goddess), to the extent that many of the rituals dedicated to her take place after sunset; *Paraśurāma Kalpasūtra* indicates explicitly that she must be adored in the middle of the night.

So among the many images of her, her vehicle (*vāhana*) may be a man on all fours (as in the temples of Paraśurāmeśvara at

---

20 *Anuttarayoga Tantra*, which can be translated as "the highest Yoga Tantra", is the way Tantric Buddhist texts of Indian origin are defined in Vajrayāna Buddhism. Traditionally they form part of the 108 volumes of *Kangyur*, the most widely recognized collection of Vajrayāna doctrinal texts.

21 A minister of the Yādava dynasty of Devagiri during the reigns of Mahādev and Rāmcandra (CE 1259-274), Paṇḍita Hemādri was also an eminent man of letters; to him we owe the alchemical text called *Caturvarga Cintāmaṇi*, as well as a medical treatise known as *Ayurveda Rasāyana*.

Bhubanesvar, of Mount Abu and Saraikela) — a clear allusion to the control-transformation of human beings into animals, an allusion reinforced by the use of *pāśa* (noose) with which Yoginī-witches bind the men who have fallen into their power. Elsewhere she rides a *gaṇa* (as in the Vaitāl Deul at Bhubanesvar, one of the rare temples dedicated to the cult of Mātṛkās), a turtle or a snake with a human head (*nāga*) — both reminders of the *pātāla* (netherworlds) — or again, a long-necked bird, in all probability a vulture.

This inclination, reflected in the name Dhūmravārāhī, the smoky black Vārāhī, is borne out in her involvement in Tantric schools of the left-hand path (Vāmācāra), which associate her cult with extreme practices such as *pañca-makāra*, which will be discussed later.

Elsewhere her name is Daṇḍa-nātha, the Lady of the rod, which in symbolic terms evokes her dominion over the axis passing through all *cakra*s of the human body, hence her command over the powers of *yoga* — that same *daṇḍa* which is a sign of royalty, but also the sceptre of Yama, Lord of death.

So Vārāhī and Cāmuṇḍā — of all Mātṛkās — seem to share some aspects typical of Tantric Yoginī cults, due to their close association with wild beasts (tigers, lions, hyenas) and birds of pretty (owls, eagles, vultures) and to their use of the *pāśa* — a symbol of possession and psychic control as well as suffocation and death — and also because of their closeness to the underworld through *preta, piśāca,* cadavers and references to Yama and *pātāla*. But beneath this extraordinary profusion of tenebrous iconographic references is hidden a much more subtle meaning.

Among the traditional sciences cited in *Chāndogya Upaniṣad,* in fact, we find *bhūta-vidyā* (science of vampires) and *sarpa-vidyā* (science of serpents, also called *gāruḍa-vidyā*). They are used along with the Veda, Itihāsa and Purāṇa during the last ten days of Aśvamedha (horse sacrifice) — a ritual of great symbolic significance — together with other dark practices like *rakṣo-vidyā* (science of evil spirits) and *asura-vidyā* (science of demons).[22] Furthermore, in *Āśvalāyana-Gṛhyasūtra*,[23] *rakṣo-vidyā* is replaced by *piśāca-vidyā*, where *piśāca* is just another name for serpents (*nāga*), sovereigns of nether regions underground (*pātālaloka*).

So these characteristics of Vārāhī and Cāmuṇḍā recall an obscure knowledge, a legacy from the gods of a previous epoch who are now relegated to the function of demons–titans–dragons (or serpents): a knowledge which is therefore extracted from the bowels of the earth to form the basis of Tantric practices.

This pairing of *nāga* with secret knowledge is central to the whole symbolic apparatus of the Yoginī, emerging also in Patañjali — the *ṛṣi* known for having divulged *rāja-yoga* (the royal or supreme *yoga*) — who is depicted with a human head and trunk and the lower body of a serpent (*fig*. 9). A transposition echoed in the tail of the *ṛṣi*, which is coiled three-and-a-half times like the spiral of *kuṇḍalinī* who, in her ophidic form, lies comfortably in the *mūlādhāra cakra* waiting to be awakened by precisely that *yoga* of which Patañjali is a master.[24]

These allusions are found also in the Daśamahāvidyā — almost all of them characterized by the *pāśa* — starting with Kālī, who in her aspect as Bhadrakālī, is surrounded by *bhūta, piśāca, yoginī, ḍākinī, yakṣiṇī* and innumerable demons, or who in the guise of Guhyakālī is visualized with a double animal and human head.

---

22 Venkateswara 1928.

23 *Gṛhyasūtra* by Āśvalāyana — a disciple of the great Ṛṣi Śaunaka — is numbered among the so-called domestic *sūtra*. These are texts which describe the rites obligatory for *gṛhasthin*, men who find themselves in the second age (*gṛhastha*) of life.

24 According to *Vāmana Purāṇa*, in order to fight the demon Raktabīja, Vārāhī emerged from the body of the Goddess seated on the serpent Śeṣanāga.

But the function of Vārāhī is not limited to such symbolic references, extending into a quite different doctrinal order. At the highest level, in fact, it is she who destroys the forces of evil which impede spiritual progress, by leading the devotee to knowledge of *śrīvidyā*. And the Śrīvidyā school itself elevates her to the rank of *parā-vidyā* (transcendental knowledge). In the same traditional setting Vārāhī, along with Kurukullā, is a constituent part of the primordial unity of Devī, assuming a function of crucial significance for the whole Śākta tradition. Finally, she is Kaivalyarūpiṇī, inasmuch as she is none other than *kaivalya* (solitude), the final goal of *yoga* and the most important of the five types of realization (*sālokya, sāmīpya, sārūpya, sāyujya* and, precisely, *kaivalya*).

Therefore, Vārāhī has the power to grant the supreme *siddhi* to those *sādhaka*s who sincerely venerate her, and for this reason she is the repository of the knowledge which opens the doors to the final *mukti* (liberation).

So if Cāmuṇḍā represents the horror of destruction, hence time the devourer, Vārāhī is the hidden knowledge, she who is capable of breaking the chains of that time. These are the two poles of the Tantric world, the essence of the left-hand (Vāmācāra) and of the right-hand paths (Dakṣiṇācāra).

However, beyond this polarization and beyond the specific connotations of Vārāhī and Cāmuṇḍā lies a symbolic significance which can only be grasped through a collective reading of the entire group of the Saptamātṛkā (*fig.* 10). So the sculptural complexes which depict them along with other figures from the Śaiva setting come to epitomize the whole trajectory of the Goddess, leading the Saptamātṛkā to embody the cosmic cycle of time and of its ending.

Here Śiva Naṭeśa, who is generally placed at the beginning of the group, starts the creation of the universe through his dance; sometimes he is replaced by Gaṇeśa, who at a subtle level represents the path of the initiate and hence the (re)birth of knowledge. Then comes the first of the Mātṛkās, who in the most classic compositions is Brāhmī, Śakti of Brahmā the creator, while Vaiṣṇavī in the centre (fourth of seven), acts as keystone of the group and alludes to the preservation of the cosmos. The cycle ends with Cāmuṇḍā — dissolution — whose skeletal appearance suggests death and, at the same time, the possibility of overcoming it. Finally Śiva reappears to set his seal on the group, now in the form of Dakṣiṇamūrti (he who pacifies the south, the reign of death), the Lord who brings knowledge, or else of Kālabhairava (he who frightens death itself). Kālabhairava is also known as Kāla-Rudra, meaning time — time which according to *Atharvaveda* is associated with a seven-part division, like the Mātṛkās (time advances with seven wheels, and seven are its hubs . . .), and whose progression signifies an inevitable appointment with dissolution. From this perspective, then, Śiva is Mahākāla, time which devours the entire universe, he who swallows everything into the great darkness. And black Kālī represents his female counterpart (*fig*. 11). But in either case, whether Śiva is Daksiṇamūrti or Kālabhairava, these figures presage the same objective: the annulment of death or, in other words, extinction of the infinite sequence of rebirths of individuals and of worlds.

Therefore the Saptamātṛkā stage a grandiose spectacle which, beginning with the creation, proceeds through the various heavens of celestial cosmology and ends with reabsorption into the primordial unity, a merging into the wild steps of Śiva as he dances to the rhythm of the flow and dissolution of universes. And Yoginīs, whose function has been shown to be complementary in terms of the mysteries to the explicit function of Mātṛkās, suggest the possibility of an interruption in — or an escape from — this perennial cycle, giving a glimpse of a door hidden in its folds. At another level they come to epitomize the secret process whereby, through knowledge of the Tantric path, ultimate liberation (*mukti*) can be attained.

3

Yoginīs as Subtle Guides

THE next category of Ḍākinīs, working down the scale implicit in Vajrayāna settings too, are spiritual beings (Vajraḍākinīs)[1] who act as guides for the practitioner. Also in the Kaula *mārga* — and more generally, in the various Śākta schools — Yoginī in subtle terms express this guiding function, presiding over diverse parts of diagrammatic representations of the sacred (*yantra* and *maṇḍala*), over syllables of the formulae (*mantra*), and all the variegated supports for Tantric ritual.

Maṇḍala or *cakra*, diagrams which summarize the structure of the cosmos, are the most widespread of these supports, and traces of them are found in the very form of the temples dedicated to the cult of the *yoginīs*. These constructions have a circular, or more rarely rectangular (*fig.* 12) plan, and they replicate — on ground consecrated by sacrifice (*vāstupuruṣa maṇḍala*) — ritual designs like *khecarī cakra* or *yoginī cakra*, both composed of sixty-four Yoginīs, *mūlādhāra cakra*, composed of eighty-one Yoginīs, or the *mālinī cakra*, composed of fifty Yoginīs.

In those *maṇḍala* painted on paper or cloth, Yoginī are

---

[1] The term *vajraḍākinī* which indicates this category of subtle guides, introduces the *vajra* (thunderbolt or diamond), a central element of Buddhist Tantra (which indeed is called Vajrayāna, the path of the *vajra*), the axial symbol par excellence and, at the same time, a sign of incorruptibility and hence of that which overcomes contingency. This symbolic perspective recurs in the names of other beings which we shall meet in the course of this study, such as Vajrayoginī, Vajravārāhī and Vajrabhairava.

arranged in a radial pattern so as to connect the circumference with the centre (*fig*. 13), in accordance with one of the most significant metaphors of Indian thought whereby the external circle represents manifestation, the world of multiplicity, as opposed to — or rather, complementing — the centre, which alludes to the origin, the unmoved mover of the universe. Thus the rays or spokes, in this case Yoginīs, become the paths which can lead mankind back to primordial unity, toward reunion (*yuj*, the root of *yoga* and hence of Yoginī) with the Absolute.[2]

An analogous view, although expressed in axial terms, has seven categories of Yoginīs (Ḍākinī, Rākinī, Lākinī, Kākinī, Śākinī, Hākinī and Yākinī) presiding over the seven *cakra*s of the human body which are aligned along an axis called *merudaṇḍa* (the rod of Mount Meru, the spinal column). Here their presence alludes to powers (*siddhi*s) which, with the reawakening of *kuṇḍalinī* which rises along that axis, are granted by Yoginīs in each of the lotus-*cakra* through which the practitioner ascends, in a subtle sense, until he is allowed to reach the *sahasrāra cakra* at the top of the head, the supreme lotus which opens the doorway to *mokṣa*.

The references to subtle knowledge and to devouring time which are highlighted by the two Mātṛkas — Vārāhī and Cāmuṇḍā — those who are symbolically closest to the Yoginīs — are reinforced by the characteristics of the sixth *cakra*, the *ājñā cakra*, made up of just two petals, which is considered to be the eye of knowledge and linked with the sense of eternity (*fig*. 14). This *cakra*, situated at the level of the pineal gland, in microcosmic terms represents the achievement of perfection of the human state, the centre where one receives from above the precepts (*ājñā*) of the inner *guru*.

---

2 It is interesting to note that in the representation of these *cakra*s, the Yoginīs who preside over the various sectors take the name of petals (*ḍāla*s) or rays (*āra*s), and that similarly, the seven rays or tongues of Sūrya are called his seven red sisters.

And the axis which passes through the diverse *cakra* is none other than the *suṣumṇā*, the central channel of the three subtle channels (*nāḍīs*) which pass through the human body. From a macrocosmic viewpoint, it is the axis which connects the terrestrial to the celestial centre, a further metaphor for reintegration in the Absolute.

Other symbolic levels are linked with the stations which measure out the ascent along the *merudaṇḍa*, such as the two triangles, one called Traipurā, situated at the *mūlādhāra cakra* at the base of the spinal column where *kuṇḍalinī* lies coiled up, and the other, Kāmakalā, supporting the *sahasrāra*, which together represent in microcosmic terms what has just been said about the terrestrial and celestial centres. And it is significant that the triangle at the base is also known as Kāmarūpa, sketching a first allusion to the identification of Assam (i.e. Kāmarūpa) as the centre of the world according to Tantric tradition.

The same seven Yoginīs (Ḍākinī, Rākinī, Lākinī, Kākinī, Sākinī, Hākinī and Yākinī)[3] are also connected with the seven *dhātus*, the constituent parts of the human body, corresponding to vital lymphatic fluid (*rasa*), blood (*rakta*), muscles (*māṁsa*), fat (*medhā*), bones (*asthi*), bone marrow and nerve tissue (*majjā*), and to semen and the reproductive system (*śukra*), thereby qualifying

---

[3] This list is found in *Śrīmatottara Tantra*. *Kaulajñāna Nirṇaya* offers an analogous list with a few variations in the names, the most significant being the insertion of Kusumamālinī (in place of Hākinī) as the Yoginī who swallows the semen of the practitioner, while Yakṣiṇī (replacing Yākinī) is assigned to the task of breaking his bones, Śaṅkhinī (replacing Sākinī) of extracting his bone marrow, Kākinī of taking his body fat, Lākinī of feeding on his flesh, Rākinī of drinking his blood and Ḍākinī of ripping off his skin (in this context a substitute for lymphatic fluid). As well as observing in the brutality of this ritual a formulation typical of the Vāmācāra schools, it is possibile to see in the Yoginīs' hierarchical consumption of the *dhātu* a reference to the proper progression in *haṭha-yoga* for the ascent of *kuṇḍalinī*. In this regard see White 2003.

them as the origin substances of manifestation.

Furthermore, the *yantra*s — diagrams which function as supports for meditation practices — are also associated with the Yoginīs.

Just as the levels (*āvaraṇa*s) of the *śrīyantra* are nine in number, so there are nine categories of Yoginīs (Prakaṭa, Gupta, Guptatārā, Saṁpradāya, Kulakaula/Kulottīrṇa, Nigarbha, Rahasya, Atirahasya, Parāparāti-rahasya/Parāparā-rahasya) which preside over every element of the *yantra* of the Devī (*fig*. 15) — a diagram formed by the intersection of five downward-pointing triangles (signs of the feminine principle) with four upward-pointing triangles (signs of the masculine principle). This is a representation in more complex terms of the symbolism of the *yantra* of Vajravārāhī (*fig*. 16), formed by the intersection of just two triangles with vertices pointing in opposite directions, to indicate the union of the basic principles of universal manifestation — the equivalent of what in the West is called Solomon's seal.[4]

At the centre of the *śrīcakra* sits the Goddess herself, Lalitā-

---

[4] The *yantra* of Vajravārāhī, representing the interpenetration of the masculine and feminine principles and hence the manifest world, finds an interesting limit in the figure of two cones joined at the points to form a sort of hourglass corresponding to the *ḍamaru*, the tambourine that Śiva holds in his hand. Although a first reading therefore relates to the flow of time — where Śiva, who beats the rhythm of life and death, is Lord of time the destroyer, which continually swallows up and transforms everything — we can also recognize here the two triangles of the *yantra*, which the God holds in perfect balance, no longer interpenetrating but just touching, on the brink of becoming. He is therefore Naṭarāja, who to the frenzied rhythm of *tāṇḍava* dance rules over that brink, over the narrow doorway through which flows the eternal destruction and rebirth of worlds. So it is no accident that in Tibet the *ḍamaru* is made from two skull-caps placed back to back, in Tantric memory of the indissolubility of life and death.

Mahātripurasundarī, she who among the Daśamahāvidyās embodies Śrīvidyā (the Science of the Devī), the most qualified path of the Śākta tradition.

Prapañcasāra Tantra[5] indicates that the central point (*parābindu*) of the *yantra* — the last and therefore the highest element of the meditative practice — is in turn subdivided into two parts, of which the part on the right is *bindu* (which takes the form of a sun disc), the masculine principle, *puruṣa, haṁ*, while that on the left is *visarga* (which takes the form of a sickle moon), the feminine principle, *prakṛti, saḥ*.

According to *Tantrarāja Tantra*, Vārāhī (also called Pañcamī), although she is represented in feminine form as a Devī, incarnates the "paternal principle" of Lalitā-Mahātripurasundarī, while Kurukullā-Tārā is the "maternal principle", and their union gives rise to the of the world, *haṁ-saḥ*. So Vārāhī is the new moon in opposition to the full moon of Kurukullā. And again, Vārāhī represents the illuminating aspect of Akula-Śiva (*prakāśa*), while Kurukullā is the reflection of Kula-Śakti or awareness of the Self (*vimarśa*), where light and reflection are two key categories used both in Vedāntic tradition and in Śākta gnosis to define the transition from the informal order, or the concurrence of all the possibilities of the universe, to the first productions of the formal order.[6]

---

5 It is one of the most important of the twenty-eight Āgamas — texts in the form of dialogues between Śiva and the Goddess (generally in the image of Pārvatī) — which dwells particularly on the constitutive form of *bindu*.

6 These categories are taken up again by Jñāna Khaṇḍa (16.64-70) of *Tripurā Rahasya* (*The Secret of the Goddess Tripurā*), which is considered to be one of the major doctrinal texts of the Śrīvidyā school. According to tradition, it was transcribed in its current form by Śrī Haritāyana, who condensed the original text ascribed to Paraśurāma.

Tripurā Rahasya is divided into three sections: *Māhātmya Khaṇḍa* (on →

Hence the polarization of Vārāhī and Cāmuṇḍā-Tārā recalls the two principles of manifestation *puruṣa* and *prakṛti* of the Sāṁkhya view, although here, far from representing duality, they appear to be integrated in their essential function inside *parābindu*, which is a reflection of the Goddess herself.

So Tripurasundarī becomes the endless cycle of emanation and reabsorption, while the yogic practice of meditation on the *śrīyantra* is transformed into a journey through the various levels of the cosmos and, at the same time, through the *cakra* of the human body, following a doctrinal view already found in the earliest texts of the Śrīvidyā school like *Yoginī-Hṛdaya* (*The Heart of the Yoginī*), which interprets the *śrīcakra* in terms of the expansion and contraction of the universe.[7] And it is the presence in the title of the term *hṛdaya* (heart) which constitutes a precise reference to the central point of the human being, the dwelling place of the Self which relates, at a macrocosmic level, to Brahmapura, the citadel of the gods, the celestial pole of the cosmic axis.

From all this emerges the sense that through their command over diverse orders of the cosmos, the Yoginīs represent the centrality of knowledge — a knowledge which, although it plays out in the operative context of a variety of methods, contains in essence references and allusions of a metaphysical order.

This view is confirmed in the Vajrayāna setting, where the Ḍākinī represents the final step on a path which begins with the master (*guru*), whom the adept needs to take the first

---

← ritual), Jñāna Khaṇḍa (on gnosis) and the now lost Carya Khaṇḍa (on conduct).

7 *Yoginī-Hṛdaya*, along with the *Nityaṣoḍaśikārṇava*, makes up *Vāmakeśvara Tantra* or *Vāmakeśvarīmatam* — the doctrine of the Lady of Vāmācāra — one of the most authoritative texts of the Śrīvidyā school from the point of view of Kaula. The work is made up of five chapters dealing with *yantra, mantra, mudrā* and the practices of the cult of Lalitā-Mahātripurasundarī.

step on the path of truth, and then proceeds with the support of a deity (*devatā*), and finally concludes with Ḍākinī, who offers attainment of the ultimate realization. In *Yangzab*, a text of the Dzogchen school, these interior levels are assimilated with the "three roots", where the *guru* is the transposition of Guru Rinpoche (Padmasambhava), the *devatā* (*yidam*) that of Hayagrīva and the Ḍākinī that of Vajravārāhī, an esoteric aspect of the Goddess whom we shall find again in a form of sacred geography in Pemako, the most important hidden land (*beyul*) in the Vajrayāna tradition.

4

Yoginīs as Navagraha and Constellations

ONCE again in the guise of subtle beings, the Yoginīs return in a cosmological key, taking their place at the centre of a long series of astral references.

Seven Yoginīs (Maṅgalā, Piṅgalā, Dhānyā, Brāhmarī, Bhadrikā, Ulakā and Siddhidā) are associated with the planets (*graha*) and constitute a seven-note scale of influences which alternate throughout the year. So every individual is linked at birth with a given position of the Yoginīs on astrological diagrams called *yoginī-daśā*. Similarly, their position at the beginning of pilgrimages is crucial, and sanctions their outcome — a function which is reflected, with a transposition of terms, in the reading of Yoginīs as a kind of guardians (*dvārapāla*s) who supervise the practitioner's progress along the path and determine the chances of reaching one's inner goals.

When this planetary scale includes an eighth Yoginī, Śāntakā, who corresponds to the couple Rāhu and Ketu, the eclipse and the comet — or in astronomical terms, the two lunar nodes (the two points where the moon's orbit intersects the ecliptic, that is the apparent orbit of the sun around the earth) — then their projection moves beyond the manifest world to comprehend the subtle levels of the cosmos, thereby sealing the complete correspondence between Yoginīs and *navagraha* (nine planets).[1]

---

1 The term *graha* — in addition to the planets — also means one who grasps or possesses, an attitude closely connected with the Yoginī.

On the other hand, Rāhu and Ketu — personification of the two parts into which Viṣṇu cut the serpent-*asura* Vāsuki for having drunk *amṛta-soma*, the nectar of immortality destined only for the gods — introduce a long series of myths related to beheading in the name of possession of the divine nectar, or that supreme knowledge which represents the final point on the path of the Tantric Yogins (*fig*. 17).

The two halves of the serpent, taking their place at the margins of more explicit planetary symbolism, necessarily subsume a series of meanings which play out in the contrast and complementarity of their functions. Rāhu, the severed head (*fig*. 18), is the eclipse of the moon, a doorway to the subtle world, and is associated with diverse types of poisoning, as well as mental disturbance, possession and madness. He is regarded as the son of Māyā (the Goddess's power of illusion), and therefore induces confusion and attachment. In contrast Ketu (*fig*. 19), the tail of the dragon, is the eclipse of the sun, the spiritual doorway (*mokṣakaraṇa*), and recalls the function of the Aśvins, doctors to the gods and masters of Āyurveda, since he is capable of removing the effects of snakebite or of illnesses in general.[2] This relates Ketu to Matsya and Gaṇeśa; like them, he represents original knowledge as an instrument of realization.

Poisoning and the ability to neutralize it, in other words power over illness and healing — which is tantamount to power over life and death, and is closely entwined with the struggle for possession of *soma* — will remain a central theme in the diverse aspects in which the Yoginīs reveal themselves. But like them, Rāhu and Ketu — eclipses, and therefore no more than shadows — do not explicitly embody the union resulting from

---

2 Ketu is depicted with a human trunk and the tail of a serpent-dragon. This representation, as we have seen, is equivalent to that of the *ṛṣi* Patañjali and symbolically suggests *sarpa-vidyā* (science of the serpent), knowledge which is hidden or forgotten because it is the legacy of an earlier time.

a fusion of opposites, but merely leave an evanescent trace of it.

In Gauhati (Assam) there is a rare and interesting temple dedicated to the *navagraha*, whose circular plan recalls that of Yoginī temples. The ten descents (*daśāvatāra*) of Viṣṇu are shown along its outer perimeter wall, while inside, eight *liṅga–yoni*s representing the planets are arranged around a central *liṅga–yoni* corresponding to the sun.

According to the traditions of *jyotiṣa* — the astrological science which was so prominent in Assam as to mark it with the name Prāgjyotiṣa[3] — Viṣṇu has to do with universal order, balance and harmony in the cosmos. This would justify the presence of *avatāra* on the outer wall, in full manifestation. Here, in the relation between the nine planets (*navagraha*) and the *daśāvatāra*, Kalkin — the future and final descent — there is an allusion to the hidden planet, the one not yet revealed or else, from a different viewpoint, the one that exploded at the beginning of time, which recalls the relationship between Kalkin and Hayagrīva in the transmission of knowledge from one cycle to the next. If in fact Hayagrīva, as the transcendent hypostasis of Kalkin, is he who saves the Veda from the final dissolution, at the beginning of the next cycle this god is transformed into an *asura* to be sacrificed so that Viṣṇu — now Matsya — can deliver the Veda to the new human race, thereby confirming the fall of *deva* from the preceding age to the status of *asura* (titans) in the world which follows. Furthermore, this corresponds to the symbolic identification of the master with an *asura* whose hidden knowledge must be coaxed from him, a reversal necessary because any initiatory — and therefore secret — teaching always

---

[3] *Jyotiṣa* furthermore means light — or by extension, ray of light — and therefore knowledge, confirming once again the function of Assam as a centre of subtle knowledge and, as we shall see further on, a point on the earth's surface onto which the cosmic axis (ray) is projected.

implies a violation of that very secrecy.[4]

If, on the other hand, the planets refer to Śiva, then they suggest the force of transformation and dissolution of the universe, of becoming. Therefore the nine *liṅga–yoni*s stand inside the *garbhagr̥ha*, the mountain cave, the place where transformation may take place through ritual. In this case the hidden planet is found at the end of the chimney which rises through the *vimāna* (tower over the central chapel), establishing itself as the subtle apex of the axis around which everything revolves, a cosmic emptiness at the centre of the orbit of the pole stars in the precession of the equinoxes. In this sense it corresponds to Viṣṇu-pāda (Viṣṇu's foot), the footprint of the transcendent on the celestial vault, indicating the gateway to the higher heavens.

Passing from polar to solar symbolism, Sūrya, fulcrum of the *yantra* of the *navagraha*, has seven rays or flames, also called seven tongues. These tongues are his red sisters (Kālī, Karālī, Manojavā, Sulohitā, Sadhūmravarṇā, Sphulliṅginī and Viśvarūpī) or little mothers, and hence again, the Saptamātr̥kās.

The Mātr̥kā-Yoginīs recur at the centre of the archaic myth of the birth of Skanda, son of Śiva, which also involves the seven stars called Kr̥ttikā — the Pleiades[5] — and the seven celestial

4 Filippi 1996. This idea recurs in the myth of Dadhyañc who is beheaded by Indra as a punishment for having divulged initiatory teachings to his disciples, the Aśvins.

5 Skanda also functions as a god of the zodiac in the form of Maṅgala (planet Mars), from which derives his role as god of war; his appellation Kārttikeya confirms his close relationship with the constellation of the Pleiades (Kr̥ttikā). Among his many names, he is known in southern India as Murugan, which name recalls the tribal god Murugu whose cult — cited in the Saṅgam literature — was celebrated in the woods or fields by priests who were not brāhmaṇa (*velan*). These rituals, along with bloody sacrifices, included Veriyaaṭṭu, a form of dance which induced trance and which is still practised today in ceremonies dedicated to Murugan.

rivers, the *sapta-sindhu*. The myth relates that the semen emitted by Śiva, distracted from Pārvatī during his *tapas*, was so ardent that it could be retained neither by Agni nor by the Gaṅgā where it had been spilled. So the six sons born in the Gaṅgā were transported to the skies of the Kṛttikā, and Pārvatī herself fused them into a single boy with six heads (the seventh star).[6]

In the heat of *tapas*, a heat which then transforms itself into the burning semen of the gods — which is not incidentally a sign of the great *yogin* — we find an allusion to knowledge so elevated as to incinerate. This reading finds an echo in the adoption of Skanda by the Kṛttikā, a constellation related to that of the Great Bear — the Saptarṣi — which in turn is the abode of immortality, the treasure chest in which knowledge of the Veda is preserved, to be transmitted from one epoch to another.

According to a variant of the same myth, the boy Skanda is first fought against and then adopted by the seven mothers *lokamātā-bālagraha* (destroyers of children), to whom he delegates the power to inflict illnesses on children under the age of sixteen, in yet another representation of the theme of mastery over life and death as a metaphor for knowledge.[7]

---

6 The Pleiades are also linked with the erection of the Vedic altar, which is made up of seven layers of bricks, thereby forming the foundation of the ritual of sacrifice.

7 This terrible limit of sixteen years reappears in the myth of Mārkaṇḍeya; at just that age Yama, or death, was supposed to reclaim the youthful *ṛṣi* for himself. But Mārkaṇḍeya appealed to Śiva and was snatched from his destiny by the god, becoming an immortal. So Śiva presents himself as Lord of life and death or, more precisely, as Yamāntaka, He who is able to vanquish death.

The same theme appears in the Vajrayāna sphere in the trumpet (*kanlin*) used as a support in certain Tantric rituals, which is made from the left femur bone of a sixteen-year-old girl.

In fact, sixteen is the age of full development of the individual and for this reason, the age at which the Goddess Tripurasundarī is represented in her perfect beauty. So sixteen years constitutes →

So through the cult of the *bālagraha* the boy Skanda came to be associated with the Saptamātr̥kā to such an extent that in their most ancient representations he completed the group, before being replaced in later periods by Gaṇeśa or Śiva himself. And in *Vāmana Purāṇa*, Skanda offers another "celestial" link with the Mātr̥kā-Yoginīs because he accompanies them when they assume the form of birds and take flight in the skies.

Vārāhī, to whom the 23rd chapter of *Tantrarāja Tantra* is dedicated, also lends herself to a doctrinal reading in a cosmological key. Her four alchemical elements (*dhātu*) are known as the four fires, symbolized in the *śrīyantra* by triangles pointing upwards. Her counterpart is Kurukullā, whose alchemical elements are the five *śakti*s, represented by triangles pointing downwards.

In turn the four "masculine" flames of Vārāhī relate to the twelve (4 x 3) solar *kalā*s or the twelve sidereal constellations (*rāśi*s), while the five "feminine" *śakti*s of Kurukullā are connected with the fifteen (5 x 3) lunar *kalā*s or the fifteen days of the waxing moon.

And it is the Nityās which constitute one of the essential elements of the Tantric cult of the Goddess; evidence for their esoteric meanings is found in numerous texts like *Bhavana Upaniṣad, Daksiṇāmūrti Saṁhitā, Jñānārṇava Tantra, Paraśurāma-Kalpasūtra, Mātr̥kācakra Viveka* and *Vāmakeśvara Tantra* (in the section called Nityaṣoḍaśikārṇava — the ocean of the tradition of the sixteen divine Nityās) (*fig*. 20).

According to *Tantrarāja*, among the various Nityās the tenth — Nityā Nityā — rules over Ḍākinī, Rākinī, Lākinī, Kākinī, Sākinī, Hākinī and Yākinī, that is the Śakti-Yoginī of the *dhātu*s (the seven vital elements which make up the human body). The

← the threshold beyond which one symbolically achieves full self-realization with the rediscovery, or rather the identification, of one's own divine nature.

eleventh — Nīlapatākā Nityā — rules over the *yakṣiṇī* and the sixty-four *ceṭaka* (servants of Śiva connected with the elements) and grants *siddhi* to the *sādhaka*.

The fifteen visibile Nityā lead to the full moon (*pūrṇamāsī*) during the fifteen nights of lunar light, when they have completely left the house of the sun, while the fifteen nights of the dark moon terminate in the new moon (*amāvasyā*), when they all re-enter this house. Along with the hidden sixteenth Nityā, subtle source of the light of all the other fifteen (*fig*. 21), they constitute the symbolic support for the doctrinal peak of the cult of the Goddess, who in this sixteenth Nityā becomes transcendent, in allusion to the metaphysical heights of the Vedānta.

It is the period of fifteen nights of the dark moon terminating in *amāvasyā* which embodies *kuṇḍalinī* asleep at the base of the *merudaṇḍa*. From here the adept sets out on his quest, following the path of the hero (*vīra*), unveiling the secrets which reside at each level or *cakra* until he reaches the threshold of the thousand-petalled lotus found at the crown of his head. From this point he can follow the path of his ancestors back to the *mūlādhāra cakra* to enjoy the full realization of his desires (*kāmya*) or else, if he has the right qualities, he can attain the level of the *divya* to whom are revealed the ultimate realities of the manifest and the non-manifest.[8] For this reason Śrīvidyā is called the science of

---

[8] Rao 2005b. These two views of the initiatory quest during the adept's lifetime correspond to what traditionally happens after death: if the deceased has reached the lunar heaven following the path of the fifteen nights of the dark moon, he can return to earth following the path of the ancestors (*pitṛyāna*), whereas if he has arrived there via the path of the fifteen nights of lunar light, he can go beyond the lunar heaven following the path of the gods (*devayāna*). Therefore the moon, where the germs of all formal possibilities dissolve and are conserved, functions as a watershed both for the destination of the path after death and, from a metaphysical perspective, between the states of formal and informal manifestation.

the phases of the moon. While Kaula methods limit themselves to the fifteen visible Nityā, whose orbit at the microcosmic level is located at the summit of the *ājñā cakra*, and whose expression is the *pañcadaśī mantra* (fifteen-syllable *mantra*) of the Goddess, in the Dakṣiṇācāra or Samaya schools this is completed by a sixteenth syllable (*śrīṁ*), thereby becoming that *ṣoḍaśī mantra* which constitutes Her secret name, and also the moon itself, enthroned at the centre of the *sahasrāra cakra*.

And in fact the sixteenth Nityā or sixteenth syllable implies attainment of the completeness that is reflected in the sixteen years of *Tripurasundarī*, and which therefore marks the transformation of the individual — a transformation which that age symbolically suggests — that is actualized by recitation of the *ṣoḍaśī mantra*.[9]

Finally, the sixteen lunar *nityā-kalā* hold the essence of the *kālacakra*, one of the principal Vajrayāna teachings of which traces are found in a text called *Tantrarāja Tantra*, which shows once again how Buddhist and Hindu viewpoints coincide in a Tantric perspective.

Although they are rarely found in places of worship, a

---

9 The sixteen Nityās, which are equivalent to the sixteen syllables of the *śrīvidyā mantra*, find a further correspondence in the cosmological diagram of the Goddess, the *śrīyantra*, where they are variously identified with the sixteen outer petals of the lotus, with the eight inner petals (in groups of two syllables), or with the successive crowns of triangles, taken to refer to diverse combinations of vowels and syllables of the *mantra*. Moreover Kurukullā, who as we have seen is assimilated with the *nityā*, presents the same symbolism in a Vajrayāna setting: in Tibetan, in fact, she is called Ku-ru-ku-le or Ri-bYed-ma, she who causes knowledge. She is represented as a sixteen-year-old girl with red skin indicating her magical power, as mentioned in n 7. Her attributes, like those of Tripurāsundarī, are the noose (*pāśa*), the bow made from a stick of sugar cane (*īkṣu-daṇḍa*) and arrows of flowers. She dances on a corpse and represents the perfection of knowledge (Prajñāpāramitā).

significant representation of the Nityās can be found in the temple of Tripurasundarī at Paramahaṁsī (Madhya Pradesh) — recently built in the *āśrama* of Śaṅkarācārya of Jośīmaṭha and Dvārakā — which once again proposes the cult of diverse aspects of the Goddess in a Vedāntic environment. Here the sixty-four Yoginīs are found lined up along the inner walls of the *mandira*. Therefore the icon (*mūrti*) of Tripurasundarī, at the centre of the circle, is found in the place corresponding to the seat occupied by Bhairava in Yoginī temples — an allusion to the union of Śiva–Śakti which is realized in the *sahasrāra cakra*, the highest point of the practitioner's path to liberation.

In a cloister built against the back of the construction we find the sixteen Nityā, accompanied by four other figures of profound symbolic significance. The group begins with a sculpture of Ādi Śaṅkara — the most authoritative interpreter of the Advaita Vedānta — flanked by Gaṇeśa, a God linked with intellectual and initiatory knowledge, opening on to a hemicycle in which are placed the various Nityās. The juxtaposition of Gaṇeśa and Ādi Śaṅkara, as well as confirming the sphere of knowledge to which the entire representation refers, recalls one of the versions of the origin of *Saundaryalaharī*, a Tantric poem composed by a great master which according to tradition, was carved on the wall of Mount Meru by Gaṇeśa himself and read there by the sage Gauḍapāda, who subsequently transmitted its contents to Śaṅkara.[10]

The group of the Nityā of Paramahaṁsī is framed on the opposite side by a statue of Mātaṅgī, Goddess of the full moon

---

10 Although the verses of *Saundaryalaharī* celebrate the grace, beauty and generosity of Pārvatī–Dākṣāyaṇī, at the same time they expound certain fundamental teachings of Śākta Tantrism such as the function of *kuṇḍalinī*, of *śrīyantra* and of the Nityā. In particular the references to Śrīkānta and Śivayuvatī, the triangles which form the *śrīcakra*, are found in the eleventh *śloka* of the section known as Ānandalaharī, the one directly revealed to Śaṅkara through divine intervention.

who was born *cāṇḍāla* (untouchable) — she who more than any other of the Daśamahāvidyā draws strength from sexual practices, although her cult at the same time can give direct access to Tripurasundarī — and terminates with the statue of Vārāhī, who implies a transposition in subtle terms of the knowledge incarnate in the great Śaṅkara who, with perfect architectural symmetry, stands exactly opposite to her. Their presence is by no means accidental because Mātaṅgī (also called Mantriṇī, the advisor, or Śyāmalā, the dark one) and Vārāhī (or Daṇḍa-nātha, the lady of the *daṇḍa*, she who commands its forces) represent in the Śrīvidyā school the two principal divinities flanking Tripurasundarī. But here the combination of Vārāhī with Mātaṅgī also suggests a kind of overlapping or equivalence between Mātaṅgī and Cāmuṇḍā, leading to a series of reflections on the relations between peaceful aspects of the Goddess (which as we shall see, unfold in the characteristics of Vārāhī–Śītalā) and irate aspects (typical of Cāmuṇḍā–Mātaṇgī–Manasā) which form the basis of the Tantric dyad of knowledge-sacrifice.

This is, therefore, a richly allusive representation to which we will return later, in an attempt to understand an opening towards the Śrīvidyā tradition, with all its tribal connections, which at this point in the cycle is occurring in the context of the most exclusive and elevated Indian metaphysical thought of the Advaita Vedānta.

5

Yoginīs as Intermediate Beings

BELOW the Yoginīs who preside over supports for meditation practices such as *yantra*, *cakra* and *nityā*, there is a world of intermediate beings who dwell in forests, ponds, caves and mountains, traces of whom have always been found in local village cults.

The Mātṛkās — who, as we have seen, are closely related to the Yoginīs — also reside in such places, which links them with the *grāmadevatā-bālagraha* and, even further back in time, with the *yakṣiṇī*, sylvan fertility gods deeply rooted in archaic India who inhabit the indistinct borderlands between the original chaos of the forest and the first clearings where Vedic sacrificial altars were erected to bring order to the world (*fig*. 22).

The continuous transmission of these elements between the Tantric and the tribal spheres is confirmed by the fifth *paṭala* of *Yoginī Tantra*, in which Śiva himself offers instructions for a great *sādhanā* involving the fifteen Kālī Nityā, to be conducted in a cremation ground, at a crossroads, in the desert, on a mountain or riverbank or at the base of a *bilva* tree. Again, *Kathā-Sarita-Sāgara* mentions rites to be conducted in cemeteries with the specific aim of attracting the *yakṣiṇī*.

Of course, crossroads are assimilated with cemeteries inasmuch as they are marked by the presence of a tumulus, a place of burial which has fallen into oblivion.[1] They constitute a

1 In fact, the role of the ancestor whose ashes were placed in the mound gradually passes from that of tutelary god of a family to →

point of attraction for unquiet spirits like *bhūta*, *vetāla* and *piśāca*, ominous presences to be placated by bloody oblations. And it is precisely at the crossing between two roads, inevitably by a tree, that we find altars dedicated to the Mātr̥kās for the immolation of *bali* (sacrificial animals), following a custom whose antiquity is testified by *Bhāsa*'s *Daridra Cārudatta* and Śūdraka's *Mr̥cchakaṭika*.

Therefore if, as Coomaraswamy[2] suggests, Mātr̥kās, Yoginīs and Ḍākinīs were originally none other than Yakṣiṇīs, it is in this origin that we must look for the roots of the sacrifices and libations of meat and liquor — food favoured by *yakṣa*s and *rāksaṣa*s — which subsequently became part of tribal cults on the one hand and Tantric rituals on the other.

So trees with their leafy crowns, fissures in tree trunks and the hollows between their roots are the places which harbour Yakṣiṇīs, Yoginīs and Mātr̥kās. According to *Kulārṇava Tantra*[3] the Yakṣiṇīs live in trees called *kulavr̥kṣa*.[4] And it is in these same trees that the Kula-Yoginīs dwell, so that the *Śāktānandataraṅgiṇī* gives the warning not to sleep under their branches or harm them in any way.[5] And *Kāśyapīya Śilpaśāstra*, in describing the characteristics of Saptamātr̥kā, relates each one to a specific type of tree, most of which are *kulavr̥kṣa*.

← protection of a clan or village, eventually becoming even more depersonalized as a "genius loci".

2 Coomaraswamy 1980.

3 *Kulārṇava Tantra* (Ocean of Kula) is the principal text of the Tantric Kaula school. It centres on Ūrdhvāmnāya, or superior tradition, one of the five elements of the doctrine symbolized by the upper face of Śiva, whose other four faces correspond to the four cardinal directions.

4 *Kāmeśvara Tantra* lists eight types of *kulavr̥kṣa* (*kula* trees): *śleṣmataka, karañja, nimba, aśvattha, kadamba, bilva, vaṭa* and *aśoka*. *Tantrasāra*, on the other hand, lists ten, with the first seven of the above list followed by *udumbara, dhātrī* and *ciñca*.

5 Eliade 1954.

These trees are laden with symbolic meanings, and constitute psychic islands of refuge for subtle beings where relations can be established with the chthonic and celestial spheres. Among them the *aśvattha* or *pīpala* (sacred fig) is the tree which above all others is identified with that function, so much so that it may be depicted with its roots — a symbol of the beginning — at the top and its branches at the bottom (*fig*. 23), to represent the manifest universe.[6] Hence the tree-axis indicates the possible descent of divine influence, but also the way back up, an ascending route opened by means of blood sacrifice.[7] This is confirmed in tribal environments in north-eastern India where goats, sheep and buffalos are sacrificed near an *aśvattha* in honour of Vanadurgā (Durgā of the forest, one of the hypostases of Kālī) and her twelve children.[8]

---

6 This image recurs in *Kaṭha Upaniṣad* where the world is compared with an eternal fig tree (*aśvattha sanātana*). According to *Bhagavad-Gītā* its leaves are the hymns of the Veda and hence whoever knows it, knows the Veda (*Bhagavad-Gītā* XV.1).

7 The ritual counterpart of *aśvattha* is the *śamī*, a female tree which functions as a womb or lap, whereas *aśvattha* represents the axis and therefore the masculine principle. Precisely in the sense of a womb or lap, *śamī* is chosen to shelter terracotta urns containing the ashes of the dead among its branches, in the hollows of its trunk or the cavities between its roots, indicating the possibility of rebirth after death. On this subject, see Filippi 1999.
It was behind a corpse exposed between the branches of a *śamī* tree that the Pāṇḍava hid their arms–sacrificial instruments during the last year of their exile in the country of the Matsya. And this last year of hiding in the forest before being restored to their regal status corresponds in effect to a post-mortem gestation, which takes us back to the function of the *śamī* described above.

8 Eliade 1954. It is noteworthy that *aśvattha* is also the name of the sacrificial pole to which the horse is tied during Aśvamedha ritual, which makes explicit the relationship between *kulavṛkṣa* and the cosmic axis.

Finally in *Kulacūḍāmaṇi*,[9] Śakti herself indicates the need to purify oneself through the acquisition of knowledge (*jñāna-śuddhi*) by means of specific practices, starting with an invocation (*praṇāma*) in front of a *kula* tree.

So the tree, and the altar placed against it, become the background or stage where humankind has always enacted the ritual of oblation in an attempt to win over Yakṣiṇīs, Yoginīs, and Mātṛkās — but also *nāga*, *ahasta* (without hands), *apada* (without feet) and other categories of subtle beings[10] — to act as guides to the worlds which extend beyond the hazy confines of the tangible (*fig*. 24).

All these worlds are stacked along the axis of the tree or of the *yūpa* (pole) — its sacrificial substitute — so that it is transformed into the long ladder scaled by the spirit of the shaman, or the cosmic axis which the *yogin* ascends thanks to the *siddhi* of flight. In this sense the tree is linked with the crossroads, the tumulus and the pond in the sacred geography of the *tīrtha* (ford), the subtle gateway between contingent reality and other-worldly dimensions. A place where one simultaneously attains the experience of a return to the state of true manhood (*vīra*) and of transformation into transcendental man (*divya*). This symbolic model is presented again in macrocosmic terms in the relation between lake and sacred mountain (another pairing of uterus and axis), as seen in some of the most venerated natural sanctuaries of the Hindu, Vajrayāna and Bon-po traditions in the coupling of Kailāsa-Mānasarovara and Amne Machin-Kokonor.

---

9 *Kulacūḍāmaṇi Tantra* is a *nigama*, that is a text in which it is not Śiva who responds to the questions of the Devī (*āgama*), but vice versa. Here the principal Goddess is Mahiṣāsuramardinī, who in seven short chapters expounds the essence of her cult, giving details of the diverse *siddhi*. She grants boons, including that mysterious process whereby the *sādhaka* abandons his body during the night for an erotic encounter with the Śakti.

10 Filippi 2006.

Furthermore, the link between the Devī and the *tīrtha* is confirmed in *Brahmāṇḍa Purāṇa* where Tārā-Kurukullā is Naukeśvarī, the Lady of boats, who saves those who are shipwrecked and metaphorically helps the practitioner to cross the ocean of existence.[11] Thus the boat is the ark built by Manu to ferry humanity from one cycle to the next, and in this light the Goddess is she who presides over that voyage, the guide we rely on to break the bonds of contingency.

Finally, to come full circle, it should be emphasized that the function of the *tīrtha* reappears, transposed, in another characteristic of the Yakṣiṇī. Along with the *yakṣa*, in fact, they are beings under the dominion of Kubera, one of the four guardians of the cardinal directions (*lokapālas*), specifically he who presides over the north, or celestial direction. As such they exercise a benign or rather a propitious function, since they safeguard the nine treasures (*navanidhi*) hidden in the earth[12] — a theme which recalls Padmasambhava and the *ter-ston* (discoverers of treasure) in the Vajrayāna tradition, as well as the *nāga*, who have always been linked with the secret knowledge hidden in the bowels of the earth.

All of this, in more general terms, suggests the hiding of wealth-knowledge underground or under the ocean, which must be recovered — one of the functions of Vārāhī — in order to regain the lost pathway leading beyond the present world. In this perspective Yakṣiṇī and Yoginī hold the keys to the treasure of hidden knowledge, a knowledge needed to cross the *tīrtha* of individual existence and reach the shores of *mokṣa*.

---

11 Schwarz 2009.

12 The nine treasures, from an alchemical point of view, find a cosmological correspondence in the *navagraha*. In this perspective the first two — *padmā* and *mahāpadmā* — are linked with two Himalayan lakes at the bottom of which precious minerals and jewels are found. This relates to the theme of the weapon hidden in the lake-womb which we will encounter in the myth of Dadhyañc, to be discussed later in the book.

6

Human Yoginīs

In human form, the Yoginīs once again show evidence of a dual nature.

They may be practitioners of *yoga* or adepts of the Kaulamārga Tantric school, but they may also take on the nature of witches and sorcerers.[1] Both of these modalities are characterized by the acquisition of powers (*siddhi*), through learning and the development of certain techniques, in the first case, or through diabolical rituals in the second.

As practitioners of *yoga*, the Yoginīs frequent forests and wild places where they dedicate themselves to long periods of asceticism (*tapas*). Thanks to the *siddhi* acquired in this way, they are able to subjugate and control wild beasts, which become their companions and guardians of their hermitages. Such powers are rendered in iconographic terms by a tiger or lion lying at their feet, or posed in reverent homage among the leafy branches of a wood.[2] More commonly *yogī* and *yoginī* — whether Hindu or Vajrayāna Buddhist — are shown seated on tiger skins. In allegorical terms, this means they have undertaken a path to realization accompanied by the appearance of powerful *siddhi*, where dominion over wild beasts constitutes an immediate

---

1 References to these circles are frequent in ancient Indian literary tradition, and traces can be found in various texts such as *Uttamacaritra-Kathānaka*, *Kathā-Sarita-Sāgara*, *Rājataraṅgiṇī*, *Mālatīmādhava*, *Vetālapañcaviṁśatī* and *Daśakumāracarita*.

2 See for example, the miniature in the Salarjung Museum in Hyderabad, published in Dehejia 1986: 11-12.

metaphor for control over the passions, the first, necessary step on the yogic path (*fig*. 25).

This symbolism finds direct confirmation in the tiger skin which Śiva himself, as the Lord of *yoga*, usually wears wrapped around his loins. A tableau from the myth from which this iconographic characteristic derives seems particularly significant: Śiva was called upon to intervene in a group of *ṛṣis* gathered in the forest of Taragam who, thanks to their long *tapas*, had accumulated such enormous powers as to upset the balance of the entire universe. Descending to earth to re-establish cosmic order, the God was attacked by a tiger which the *ṛṣis* had generated from the sacrificial fire of their *siddhi*. But with the nail of his little finger, *Śiva* killed the beast and skinned it, wrapping the tiger skin around his flanks.[3]

It is not so much the outcome of this struggle which calls for our attention as the reference to powers developed in the depths of the forest, their improper use (and particularly the fact that it was actually some *ṛṣis*, custodians of knowledge, who were responsible for this inversion), and above all the emergence of

3 The myth of Śiva in the pine forest at Taragam presents innumerable variants which are extremely interesting. In one of these the God assumes the form of a nude ascetic who wanders in the forest, but his beauty unsettles the wives of the *ṛṣis* and distracts them from their practice. In another version drawn from *Mahābhārata*, Śiva appears in the forest in the guise of a Kirāta, a tribal hunter who is also naked, and there seduces outcast women. Elsewhere he enters the pine forest in the guise of a *bhikṣāṭana*, a naked beggar who, like the outcasts, wears a bell on a string round his calf, to give due warning of his impure presence. — Doniger O'Flaherty 1976.

These myths skin which at different levels deal with the erotic nudity of a divine being, his sexual relations with outcast women, or the arousal of erotic desire among Yoginīs who are the consorts of *ṛṣis*, in any case imply consequences in terms of sacrifice and will recur, with the same ambiguous role, in the myth of Reṇukā which will be examined later.

the tiger from the sacrificial fire as a first effect of the *siddhi*.[4] If therefore Śiva Naṭarāja is the Lord of the cosmic dance, the hide of a wild beast — particularly the spotted skin of the leopard — around his flanks represents the starry mantle of the sky, the sky which He populates and empties of worlds, dancing to the rhythm of his *ḍamaru*.

We may intuit that the tiger suggests something more indistinct, an allusion to the emergence of powers (conquest of the skies) once the practitioner has set out on the path of initiation, and at the same time, to that savage energy which can be used as an instrument of inner development.[5] This reading is confirmed by the tiger — or lion — acting as *vāhana* of the Goddess, thereby becoming the potent support on which she balances in her battle to suppress the buffalo-demon Mahiṣa (*fig.* 26). In subtle terms, this battle is equivalent to the destruction of darkness — and hence of ignorance and death — so that *amṛta* emerges from the severed neck of the buffalo, revealing the light concealed by appearances.[6] Hence the tiger is a support for recovering hidden knowledge, and the *yogin* who mounts it or wraps a tiger skin around his flanks is the one capable of using that knowledge.

A similar interpretation recalls the traditional environment of the Kānphaṭa *yogin* of the Gorakhnātha school, who were feared because of their magical powers and particularly because of their command over rain, snakes and ferocious animals. These are strongly allusive powers, as in the case of Hari-Siddha, a direct disciple of Gorakhnātha, who was known not only for his dominion over wild beasts, but also for the prodigious events evoked by the force of the *mantra* he recited while flying

---

4 Filippi 1978c.

5 Emphasizing the subtle function represented by these wild beasts, *kuṇḍalinī* is described as a splendid young girl seated on a lion.

6 Filippi 1993.

astride a broomstick (an obvious reference to the occult powers of witches). He was further known to have exchanged the heads of queens Adunā and Padunā (this power, linked with *pravargya-vidyā*, sanctions the idea of sacrifice-initiatory death and will be analysed later in the myth of Reṇukā), and to have descended to the underworld to recover the soul of the young king Gopicandra, snatching him from the clutches of Yama — which reintroduces the function of Yamāntaka, conqueror of death or, in other terms, the above-mentioned function of Durgā Mahiṣamardinī, who cuts off the head of the demon-buffalo.[7]

This perspective is also found in shamanic circles, where the tiger is the Lord of initiation who carries the neophyte through the jungle on his back — a transposition of the guide to the descent into the underworld, and of the experience of initiatory death.[8]

Psychic possession of a wild animal, which is transformed and subjugated to become a *paśu* (the domestic animal held by a *pāśa*, the leash or lasso that we have already encountered as an attribute of the Mātṛkās and Mahāvidyās), seems then to be a transversal characteristic of Yoginīs, whether human or divine. In this function they are close to Śiva Paśupati, Lord of the animals, whose cult is particularly widespread among Kāpālikas and Kālamukhas, ritual counterparts of the Yoginīs themselves.

Furthermore, the etymology of the word *paśu* indicates a living being restricted by some bond — a bond which from a Vedāntic perspective refers both to the human condition and to

---

7 Another disciple of Gorakhnātha, Queen Māyānamatī, is remembered for her extraordinary powers, including the capacity to cross a bridge made of a single hair and to walk along a razor's edge. As we shall see further on, such powers reappear in the ritual trances of Deoḍhā shamans during the festival of Debaddhani at Kāmākhyā.

8 Eliade 1954.

all the particular limiting conditions (*upādhis*) of being — so that Śiva Paśupati becomes the "Lord of bound beings", who through his transformative action may be liberated from individual existence. But the term *paśu* suggests a further important train of thought because it also designates the victim of a sacrifice. This ritual, through a transposition of terms, comes to mean the possibility of loosing individual bonds, connecting the victim (*yogin*) with higher states of being.[9]

The sacrifice of the self, which for the Dakṣiṇācāra schools is expressed in renunciation of one's worldly identity in order to undergo initiatory death and tread the path of knowledge, becomes explicit, albeit at a necessarily less qualified level, in certain Vāmācāra practices where the *sādhaka* inflicts wounds on himself to offer the Goddess his own blood or even fragments of his own flesh.

And it is in just these contexts, relating to the so-called left-hand paths, that we encounter Yoginīs who are Tantric adepts. Here the Yoginīs gather in circles, as seen in the sculptures arranged in rings in medieval temples, to celebrate rituals which

---

9 Guénon 1925. Gaṇeśa, like the gods considered so far (such as Vārāhī, Cāmuṇḍā and Mahāvidyā), also has the attribute of *pāśa*, which confirms his initiatory function as a vehicle of knowledge, and also a connection with sacrifice, since he himself was decapitated by Śiva.

It should also be noted that *pāśa*, a symbol of the reining in of the passions, is also one of the attributes of the Goddess Tripurasundarī, along with the elephant goad (*aṅkuśa*), which represents sloth — and, therefore, with a transposition of terms, the power of the Goddess to overcome both passion and laziness in spiritual commitment — to which should be added the stick of sugar cane (*īkṣu-daṇḍa*), that is, the bow, representing the mind (*manas*), and the five floral arrows which indicate the five elements or *tanmātra* (earth, water, fire, air and ether). These eight attributes are symbolically represented in the crown of eight triangles which surrounds the innermost triangle in *śrīyantra*.

involve immersion in the grossest elements of the body before reaching a level beyond them. The most widespread of these rituals are grouped under the name *pañca-makāra*s (five Ms) — also called *kula-tattva* or *kula-dravya* — a mass of techniques characterized by the consumption of substances which for various reasons are considered impure or inebriating, such as *matsya* (fish), *māṁsa* (meat), *mudrā* (usually an hand or body position, but also a kind of roasted cereal having aphrodisiac or, according to other sources, hallucinogenic effects)[10] and *madya* (wine), as well as practices involving sexual union, *maithuna*. In some Vāmācāra schools these elements may be sublimated to the level of bodily fluids and secretions, recalling the kind of Tantrism which sees the *sādhaka*'s body as an instrument of alchemical transformation.[11]

The obvious coarseness of all these rites is transposed in a devotional key in the figure of Bhairava, the terrible aspect of the great *yogin* Śiva, and one of the central reference points for followers of Kaula (*fig.* 27) — as seen in the position of his *mūrti* in Yoginī temples — through a cult which shares certain extreme practices with the Kāpālikas (those who bear the skull, or *kapāla*s).[12] Banquets of human flesh, the drinking of alcohol and

---

10 Ritual use of these cereals may be compared with phenomena which in medieval Europe were attributed to Satanic possession, and dealt with by witch burning. In fact, they were due to the hallucinogenic effects of bread made with horned rye, where the rye has been attacked by the fungus *claviceps purpurea*.

11 Practitioners of these schools are consequently divided between *madya sādhaka*s, whose practice involves sucking the liquid which flows from the *brahmarandhra*, *māṁsa sādhaka*, who use secretions from the tongue, *matsya sādhaka*s, who control the movement of two fish in the inner channels *iḍā* and *piṅgalā* (equated with Gaṅgā and Yamunā), *mudrā sādhaka*s who use cerebral secretions, and finally *maithuna sādhaka*s who hold back the white seed (in the case of male practitioners) and the red seed (for female practitioners).

12 Bhairava is closely connected with the idea of sacrifice in that he →

sexual coupling are carried out in cremation grounds by couples of *sādhaka*s, traditionally eight in number; the males are called Adhikārins and the females, precisely, Bhairavīs. The presence of the latter, who are normally members of low castes marked by social exclusion and thus ritual impurity — a clear allusion to Mātaṅgī, the Mahāvidyā who was born *cāṇḍāla* (untouchable) — emphasizes a reversal of the Brāhmanic perspective typical of the Vāmācāra Tantric schools.[13]

The apparent absence of confirming evidence might seem to relegate these practices to the ambit of largely extinct cults. Traces of nocturnal rituals in cremation grounds to evoke the potency of *siddhi* are nevertheless documented even today, as in the area around Kāmākhyā (Gauhatī, Assam), where an occasional observer witnessed the arrival of a tiger and some jackals in response to the call of the *sādhaka*.[14]

This indicates that the Kaula *mārga* maintains its vitality in certain areas of India — above all in peripheral areas where interaction with tribal cultures is strongest, or in places where devotion to the *Devī* is most deeply rooted. The scarcity of information about it should be ascribed to its strictly mysteric

← emerged from the fury of the God Śiva himself in order to punish Brahmā by cutting off his fifth head. On the island of Sri Lanka he is known as Bhairawa, a God who also functions as the protector of treasures, indicating the close relationship between sacrifice and hidden treasure which will be examined later.

13 Ramasso 2010. However, Dakṣiṇācāra practices are remote from this type of ritual, to the extent that the principal divinity is no longer Bhairava, but Dakṣiṇāmūrti (the Lord of *yoga* and of knowledge), which orients all the operations of this path towards the attainment of supreme knowledge.

14 This testimony was given by Śrī Tīrath Nāth Śarmā and is quoted in Dehejia 1986: 223-24. The *sādhaka*'s capacity to invoke tigers recalls what has already been said about the *siddhi* involving control over wild beasts. The jackal offers an even more specific reference in that, like the dog, it is a vehicle of Bhairava.

where similar practices still survive, stories are told of witch women who meet in the forest at the dead of night and here, completely naked, sing and dance in the company of spirits (*boṅgā*) and lions. Eliade reports the deep fear surrounding the Bez, inhabitants of the village of Mayang not far from Kāmākhyā, who are held to be capable of turning men into animals and keeping them enslaved. And the same cultural context is the source of an affirmation by a shaman who was particularly feared in the area of Tezu (Arunachal Pradesh) — collected during the VAIS mission of 2001 — that at night he would visit one of the researchers in the group in the form of a lion.

The diverse references to Yoginīs which can be traced back to shamanic origins are all present in a geographically remote story from *Liao Chai chih*, published in China in the second half of the seventeeth century.[19] Tale number 207, set in Shantung, is about the exorcism of evil spirits and tells how Manchu women used to question the spirits with the help of a soothsayer. However, this fortune teller played only a marginal role, limited to dancing and beating a drum rhythmically to induce trance in the lady of the house, on whom the entire ritual hinged. In time with the rhythm of the drum and supported by assistants, the lady would start to move on one leg only — outlining the dance known as that "of a bird on one leg" — and to murmur a monotonous chant on a continuous, unvarying note, so that none of those present was able to understand it. Suddenly the candles would be snuffed out and the lady would call out the names of the spirits of her ancestors in a loud voice. Once the candles were lit again, it would be discovered that the offerings which had previously been prepared — cuts of meat and jars of wine — had been consumed, a sign that the spirit had taken possession of the

---

19 *Liao Chai chih or Liaozhai Zhiyi* (literally *Strange Stories*) is a collection of 435 tales composed by P'u Sung-ling (1640–1715). See P'u Sung-ling 1913.

lady who at that point was able to function as an oracle.

However, if doubts arose about the interpretation of the answers received, they would move on to a second phase of the ritual where the lady of the house, sumptuously dressed, would ride on the back of a fake tiger and then dance in the centre of the room holding a lance, surrounded by other women. These women, young and old, would stand upright in a circle, "neither thinking nor feeling tired". The practice was known as "dispelling evil spirits with the tiger", and the oracle was addressed by the other women with various names of warlike divinities.

The ritual described by P'u Sung-ling contains elements typical of the trance induced by the beating of drums and dancing, and also of shamanic flight (the steps of the woman's dance), of possession (indicated by the speaking of words in an incomprehensible tongue, a clear allusion to the language of birds), of the chthonic voyage to the world of the dead and of the sacrificial offering of meat and wine. Furthermore, it is particularly interesting because it occurs in an almost exclusively female environment where the "power" arises inside a circle of women in an ecstatic state (they neither think nor feel tired), capable of invoking a divinity who manifests in a form not dissimilar to that of Durgā.

These are recurrences of practices and traditional signs found all across Asia, including some precise references to the Hindu cultural environment like the attributes of Skanda, who as god of war is the Lord of mortality, symbolized by the lance (not accidentally called *śakti*), and of immortality, symbolized by the bird — so once again the power over life and death — or else the woman possessed by a *gandharva*,[20] who in a state of

---

[20] It is precisely the *gandharva* who cause the obscuration of the mind — hence, in a certain sense, the possession — of Reṇukā, which as we shall see, leads to her being sacrificed by her son Paraśurāma. And in fact the term indicating possession by a *gandharva*, that is →

tells the story of a mother who, desperate at the loss of her two children, went deep into the forest to look for them. After wandering in the absolute darkness of the night of a new moon (as in the rituals of Dhūmāvatī), she found herself inside the walls of a temple dedicated to the Yoginī. Here, exhausted and distraught, Videhā fell to her knees and prayed until the Goddess herself appeared before her and granted the restitution — equivalent to the healing — of her children. Moreover, the woman's name, Videhā, is highly evocative in that it means outside the body, after death. This detail suggests *videha-mukti*, one of the three ways in which an individual can reach final liberation (*krama-mukti, videha-mukti* and *jīvan-mukti*), namely the liberation which may be attained at the very moment of death. The myth is perfectly suited to such a symbolic transposition in that the woman lost in the forest on a dark night — an image emblematic of death — arrives at the temple of the Yoginī, who here act as psychopomps, and thanks to the intercession of the Devī obtains reunification (*yoga o yuj*, a term which indicates precisely reunion with the Supreme, a synonym for liberation) with her children, the fruit of her life, or in other words, the ultimate aim of individual experience.[3]

Returning to our search for traces of the Yoginīs as aspects of *grāmadevatās*, in the area of Mount Girnar in Gujarat we encounter three categories of them — Lala-Yoginī, Kesura-Yoginī and Pula-Yoginī — who are invoked during outbreaks of cholera.[4] Apeśvarī, a minor divinity in Assam whose name

---

[3] Videha is also the realm of the Sage Janaka (to whom we shall return later in relation to Assam and the myth of Naraka), where ancient knowledge is preserved which has been handed down from the lost civilization of Sarasvatī. In another sense, it is the name of a king who after death was able to father children thanks to magic rites performed on his corpse (so that, as in the case of Videhā in the Yoginī Vrata, children become the fruit obtained after death).

[4] Oppert 1893.

derives from *apsaras*es (a family of celestial nymphs often associated with *gandharva*s), is in the habit of fixing her shadow to the ground; any child who incautiously treads on it will be assailed by attacks of epilepsy or of paralysis, the two polar opposites — shaking and immobility — typical of phenomena of possession. Then in Tamil areas, we find terracotta figures of seven virgins (*sapta kannimar*) which are adored on riverbanks when epidemics break out. Finally, there are seven female divinities who preside over the principal illnesses. Among these, particular devotion is reserved for Manasā (Goddess of poisoning) and for Śītalā (Goddess of smallpox).

Of all the *grāmadevatā* cults, perhaps that of Śītalā is the most powerful and widespread, so that she is found throughout India under a wide range of names such as Māri, Mari-āyī, Mariyāmman, Muṭṭu Mariyāmman, Āmman and others, including Selliyāmman (mother of responses), which connects her with the oracular function, Padmābatīmā (mother born of the lotus), an appellation also typical of Manasā, and Hārīti — a name used in Assam and the sub-Himalayan regions, whence it has filtered into the Vajrayāna tradition — indicating a Yakṣiṇī who devours children.

She is at times depicted as a naked and skeletal old woman, at others as a young woman. It is her distinctive attributes which do not vary, that is the winnowing-fan worn as a headdress, the vase full of water (or of lentils, alluding to pustules), the broom, and also the flying ass which is her mount (*fig*. 29), an animal already encountered as a sacrificial offering to Nirṛtī — a further aspect of Śītalā — and always a sign of dark forces.[5] The broom, too, in the East as in the West, recalls a certain kind of witchcraft,

[5] Filippi 2002. The diabolical inclinations of this animal (often contrasted with the celestial nobility of the ox) permeate both Eastern and Western traditions, and find confirmation in *Rāmāyaṇa* where Rāvaṇa, red king of *rāksaṣa*s, has the head of an ass, while his brother Khara has an entirely asinine appearance.

of the Goddess Manasā, is celebrated in Assam, in the sanctuary of Kāmākhyā, at fixed times of year (in the months of Jyeṣṭha, Aṣāḍha, Śrāvaṇā and Bhādra). On these occasions, a clay cast of a large-hooded snake with eight heads (*aṣṭanāga*) is placed in the temple courtyard. However, the festival is also organized outside of the canonical periods in the event of epidemics and plagues. Manasā is then invoked as Marai — with an evident juxtaposition of name and function with Mariyāmman-Śītalā — and abundant sacrifices are made to her.[12] At the heart of the ceremonies are the *deoḍhā*, twenty-one shamans dressed as various gods and goddesses of the Hindu pantheon, by whom they are possessed in the course of the ritual dances. Debaddhani reaches a peak on the third day, when only the *deoḍhā* possessed by Śakti go into a trance and dance on a long sharp blade, without receiving any injury.[13]

---

12 Sacrifices may be replaced in Dakṣiṇācāra practices by a *pūjā* on the *śālagrama* — ammonite fossils traditionally gathered on the bed of the Kālīgaṇḍakī River in Nepal — which represent the *cakra*, an attribute of Viṣṇu, and which therefore find an important ritual use in Vaiṣṇava circles. Such a substitution leads to a series of considerations beyond the scope of this study, but at least a mention should be made of the link between *śālagrama* — ammonite fossils, hence representations of the ancient *nāga* — and Muktinātha (Lord of Liberation), a sanctuary in the mountains overlooking the Kālīgaṇḍakī River, which is particularly associated with *śālagrama* cult and is the goal of one of the most important Hindu pilgrimages, offering evident correspondences between *nāga*, hidden knowledge, sacrifice and liberation.

13 As we have seen, the dance on the knife's edge constitutes a precise symbolic reference to the initiatory ordeal which recurs, among other instances, in the case of Māyānamatī, a disciple of Gorakhnātha, noted for her capacity to walk across a bridge made from a hair or to walk on a razor's edge. This recalls the perilous quest and the narrow path of many tales from the Arthurian cycles, or the Irish saga of Cu Chulainn in which the ordeal of the "bridge of leaps" involved the hero leaping up on to the bridge which then →

The symbolic complexity of the celebration is reflected also in the canonic provenance of the *deoḍhā*, six of whom traditionally come from the Kāmākhyā area while the others originate in various districts of Assam.[14] In this way Kāmarūpa becomes a metaphor for the entire celestial cosmos, which revolves around its centre, Kāmākhyā, a transposition of Brahmapura, the citadel of the gods at the summit of Mount Meru.[15]

The myth of the origin of the *deodhānī nāc* (*deodhānī* dances) tells of a king without heirs who appealed to the goddess Bhairavī for the grace of a son, promising to offer his own head as a sacrifice if his wish were granted. Some time later a boy was born, but the king forgot his vow. So one night the Goddess appeared to him in a dream to claim the offering. The pious king rose and went to the temple of Bhairavī, where he

---

← shrank to the narrowness of a hair and the hardness of a fingernail.

Dances of possession are held also in Kerala during the festivities in honour of Muvalamkuli-Cāmuṇḍī who — like Manasā — is not the principal divinity resident in the temple. During the rite the celebrant exorcises the devotee, into whom the Goddess is felt to have penetrated, attempting to capture her by means of the recitation of specific *mantra*. Once this has been achieved, she is imprisoned in a copper vessel which is hurriedly buried. The Goddess obviously manages to escape, and in a fury, sets off in pursuit of the celebrant, who has in the meantime taken refuge in a temple dedicated to Śiva. When Muvalamkuli-Cāmuṇḍī recognizes the place she has reached, she decides to enthrone herself there in order to remain by the side of the God. In this way the transition is made between the tribal divinity with her cult of possession and the Brāhmanic divinity adored in the temple. — Flood 1996

14 Mishra 2004.

15 This equivalence is reflected in the name Nīlācala (blue mountain) which distinguishes the hill on which the temple of Kāmākhyā is built, and in the blue colour of the northern side of Mount Meru, made of sapphire, facing Jambudvīpa, the continent corresponding to the current *manvantara.*

Śītalā, invoked by the faithful as *Mā*, the merciful mother, is she who can heal — which is why her name derives from *śīta*, (cold) hence "she who cools" (the excesses of fever) — but at the same time she represents that terrible force which on a whim, and following a logic which is unfathomable for her "children", provides for the spread of contagion with its burning and fever.[21]

The blazing heat of the Devī — a heat which for that matter may beset the *yogin* as an effect of *tapas* — recurs in the myth of Mariyāmman, a southern version of Śītalā, which tells how a girl of brāhmaṇa caste was tricked by his disguise into marrying an untouchable. Discovering the truth, but too late, she killed herself for shame, and then turned into Mariyāmman, in whose guise she punished the man by immolating him. There is evidence here of a Goddess who stands at the crossroads in the ritual contradistinction between brāhmaṇa and untouchables, a polarity reflected in her function as alleviator (cooler of fevers), in contrast with the punishment she dispenses by burning men to ashes.

Reṇukā, the mother of Paraśurāma, also manifests this split personality. She is an extremely interesting figure in that she sums up in herself a series of characteristics which outline the delicate and complex infusion of tribal practices and beliefs into the Brāhmanic sphere. This process is even more significant if we bear in mind that it has taken place not so much in Śaiva circles, which have always been closer to similar experiences through Tantrism, as by reproduction in a Vaiṣṇava and hence less transgressive setting.

The myth, although fragmented into innumerable versions and allusive rivulets, unfolds around the central theme where

[21] An identical meaning is found in the name of Mariyāmman, or Māriyāmman, the southern version of Śītalā, because *māri* in the Tamil language is the cooling monsoon which arrives at the very peak of the season of torrid heat, the season in which contagion usually spreads.

Reṇukā, wife of Ṛṣi Jamadagni[22] and a Yoginī in her own right, loses the powers acquired through *tapas* when she is excited by the chance sighting of a *gandharva* and an *apsaras* in amorous embrace while they bathe in a pool in the depths of the forest.[23] After returning to her husband's hut, Reṇukā's inner turmoil is betrayed by her blushing or, according to a different version, by the stench of fish she gives off[24] leading Jamadagni to believe she has not kept her vow of renunciation. So the disdainful *ṛṣi* orders his sons to sacrifice her. Of these only Paraśurāma accepts the thankless task, asking his father Jamadagni to grant him one wish in exchange for his dutiful obedience — a wish which will turn out to be that Reṇukā be brought back to life (*fig*. 31). This resurrection, however, does not absolve Paraśurāma of his guilt, which will require a long and severe atonement.

Here we find signs, not excessively veiled, which are typical of the Tantric sphere, ranging from the doctrine of sacrifice, to sexual practices, to initiatory death, to the function of *tīrtha* (the pool in the middle of the forest), to the powers acquired on the

---

22 Jamadagni, along with Kaśyapa, Atri, Vasiṣṭha, Viśvāmitra, Gautama and Bharadvāja, is one of the seven sages (*saptarṣi*) of the current *manvantara*, who are transposed in astronomic terms in the constellation of the Bear, the celestial ark in which the Veda are conserved.

23 See again the comments on *gandharvamādana* in n 20, Chap. 6.

24 The stench of fish is an image leading to a variety of extremely interesting considerations about relations between the element of water and transformation of the individual. Apart from the well-known echoes of the figures of mermaids-*nāginī* who can be freed from their earlier condition by marriage to a human being, which makes possible rebirth in the body of a beautiful maiden, it is also worth mentioning the cyclic function of the fish (*matsya*) and the powers linked with the reawakening of *kuṇḍalinī* and in this perspective, the Tantric practice of the two fish which are controlled by the *matsya sādhakas* in their movements along the internal *nāḍī* — *iḍā* and *piṅgalā*.

yogic path. In particular the loss of those powers — hence a cooling — is rendered in opposite terms in that Reṇukā blushes — she becomes hot — because of the impurity of what she saw. It is just this inversion which seems extremely significant at the symbolic level because it implies the intervention of Kāma, who is capable of arousing dormant sexual energy or, in other terms, the reawakening of *kuṇḍalinī*, a preparation for the true Tantric initiation of Reṇukā, which will take place through her sacrifice.

However Kāma, too, is a victim of the heat he himself provokes in that he was "turned to ashes" by Śiva for wanting to instil in the God a desire to unite with Śakti. Along with the classic reading of this immolation as a punishment — a punishment immediately emended by Śiva's own resurrection of Kāma — we find ourselves in the presence of the tremendous heat of the energy of manifestation, a heat of which the flames of erotic desire are a mere reflection, as confirmed by the unbearable heat of the scorching sperm of Śiva in the myth of the birth of Skanda. This generative fury finds a counterpart in the watery fury of the Goddess when Gaṅgā must be reined in, again by Śiva, because her vehemence would have devastated the earth. So here we have a recurrence of some of the most common symbolic correspondences of the cyclic beginning of manifestation which plays out in the pairing of *puruṣa* and *prakṛti*, sun and moon, heat and water, light of knowledge and elixir of immortality.

It is not by chance that Kāma is assimilated with Agni, or fire, the epitome of heat and luminosity, but above all of transmutation in the ritual offering, the offering invoked in the most sacred funerary *mantra* in India, *rāma nāma satya hai* (the name of Fire is truth), in which the *mantam* of fire, *rāma*, a homophone of the God Rāma, suggests the husband of Reṇukā whose name Jamad-Agni is a synonym for sacrificial fire and thus by extension, for *kravyād*, devourer of the raw, the fire which consumes the flesh on the funeral pyre. Hence Jamadagni, like

Kāma, appears as an agent of sacrifice, the sacrifice of which his son Paraśurāma (Rāma with the *paraśu* or axe) is the instrument.

And it is precisely Kāma in his role as psychopomp, the one who creates the conditions for passage to another state — thereby functioning as a *tīrtha* — who is at the centre of one of the most evocative passages in *Vāmakeśvarīmatam* (IV.45-46):

In the place of Kāma,
which is at the centre of Kāma and in the middle of Kāma,
one should fashion a hole.
Through Kāma one should accomplish Kāma,
And should place Kāma within Kāma.
Having become lovers of Kāma,
in the place of Kāma one can shake the world.

So there is a continual exchange of functions between Rāma–Paraśurāma, Agni–Jamadagni and Kāma–Reṇukā, who delineate at diverse levels the trinity of sacrificer, sacrificial instrument and sacrificial offering.

However, a variety of narrative digressions are grafted on to these structural elements of the myth, which tend to lead the story of Reṇukā back to a shamanic or tribal ambit.

So one of the many versions of the beheading tells how, in an effort to escape the axe wielded by her son, she escapes into the forest where she meets an untouchable woman. When Paraśurāma reaches her, Reṇukā embraces the impure woman so that the axe blow severs both of their heads. When Paraśurāma is later granted by Jamadagni the wish that his mother be brought back to life, a mistake occurs and Reṇukā's head is put back on the body of the untouchable woman — who will be adored as Mariyāmman — while the head of the impure woman is placed on to the body of Reṇukā, becoming Ellammā (or Yellammā), a goddess particularly venerated in the Deccan and in the south of India as the patroness of the tribal and untouchable *Dalit*.[25]

---

[25] Such a substitution and repositioning of previously decapitated →

So the figure of Reṇukā is broken down into Mariyāmman–Śītalā, leading us back to what has recently been noted about the Goddess of smallpox, and into Ellammā–Yellammā, one of the Mātṛkā of tribal origin with strong sexual connotations, introducing the characteristics typical of Mātaṅgī which will be considered shortly. And it is in this last guise, in the intertwining of sacrifice and Tantric sexual practices, that the function of the *devadāsī* — courtesans dedicated to ritual prostitution, who are traditionally found in temples consecrated to the Goddess Yellammā — can be understood.

So in the mortal embrace between Reṇukā and the untouchable woman, and in the horror of the regenerative exchange of heads we may recognize, from a somewhat unexpected Vaiṣṇava[26] angle, convergences and juxtapositions between Brāhmanic and tribal cults or, according to an equivalent reading, between the Tantric right-hand path (Dakṣiṇācāra), with its ritual purities, and the left-hand path (Vāmācāra), with the teachings of Kaula-mārga and the darker practices of *pañca-makāra*.[27]

← heads suggests the science of *pravargya-vidyā* which, as we shall see, is closely connected with the highest knowledge, *madhu-vidyā*, the path which leads to liberation.

26 This perspective is actually not so rare, since in Assam the Tantric Vaiṣṇava sect of the Barkheliya (or Pūrṇadhāriyā) is still found today, widespread mostly among untouchables, and its adepts make large use of *pañca-makāra* practices, while in Orissa — again in tribal areas — one finds constant overlapping between sylvan and Buddhist, Vaiṣṇava and Śākta cults, as well as the persistence of a devotion to Paraśurāma mixed with devotion to Durgā-Kālī, heavily characterized by bloodthirsty rituals. — Beggiora 2009

27 The same overlapping reappears in Odisha in a *Śaiva* context when, from the tenth century onwards, with the decline of the Pāśupata cult and the establishment of Śāktism, representations of Ekapādamūrti — the first of the Ekādaśa Rudra — started to develop even more terrible characteristics and became associated with the yoginī. — Ramasso 2004

The same symbolic structure emerges in Mātaṅgī (*fig*. 32), certainly one of the most singular hypostases of the Devī and whose interpretation is most obscure. While remaining part of the Daśamahāvidyā, and hence of the most qualified and elevated circle of the Śākta doctrine, she was born *cāṇḍāla* (untouchable). This is confirmed by her name, which alludes both to her exclusion from purity of caste and to her belonging to the tribal world as a savage inhabitant of the mountains. For this reason she is associated with Śiva Mataṅga, an aspect of the God venerated by the Śabaras or Śavaras — tribal populations of the Vindhya mountains, while a different tradition links him with the Kirātas, a people of Himalayan stock who have settled in north-eastern India.[28] Śabaras and Kirātas are in turn closely linked with the cult of Kāmākhyā, whose temple on the hill of Nīlācala, in Assam, is surrounded by chapels consecrated to the various Daśamahāvidyā, so that rites of tribal origin find their place at the heart of the cult of the Goddess.

In her aspect as Ucchiṣṭa-Cāṇḍālinī, Mātaṅgī amplifies these tendencies, juxtaposing social exclusion (Cāṇḍālinī, she who was born *cāṇḍāla*, untouchable) with a further element of impurity, since *ucchiṣṭa* is the morsel of food left over after it has touched the mouth, but also the ashes (the leftovers) of sacrifice. She is therefore the incarnation of the most extreme rites of *pañca-makāra* involving the consumption of impure food and drink and also sexual union, which from the Vāmācāra Tantric viewpoint become objects of practice suitable for the hero (*vīra*), the only one capable of facing the dangers of a *sādhanā* whose effects are potentially devastating.

The Śrīvidyā school, the maximal doctrinal expression of Śāktism, proposes the same duality in a Brāhmanic context. Thus the practices of *pañca-makāra* devised to reawaken *kuṇḍalinī* are followed on both paths. However, while the grossness and impurities of the Vāmācāra path oblige initiates — especially

[28] Ramasso 2010.

those of high caste — to maintain secrecy and to conceal their practice of such rites from their social milieu, the Dakṣiṇācāra path provides for the substitution of various practices with symbolic equivalents (*pratinidhi*), such as the offering of milk instead of wine, sesame instead of meat and fish, and flowers in place of sexual union.[29] In any case *pañca-makāra* maintains its connection with *mr̥tyu* (death) — yet another "M" — as a hidden or ultimate element of the ritual in the form of sacrificial death or initiatory death, as is incidentally confirmed by the presence of sesame as a symbolic replacement for meat.

Returning to the myth of Reṇukā, another version relates that her severed head rolled far away from her body, as far as a place inhabited by *ādivāsī* and hence — because it was impure — out of reach for Jamadagni, who therefore could not honour his promise to Paraśurāma to bring his mother back to life. To make amends, at least in part, the *r̥ṣi* arranged for the head (*fig*. 33) — Māyārūpa (form of Māyā) — to become the object of the cult of Ellammā, Yellammā or Ekavīra (solitary hero). This last name is a clear allusion to the heroic tendencies — that is, the tendency to overcome all fear in the use of elements considered impure and consequently dangerous — which must be possessed by whoever undertakes the Tantric path.

The rolling of the decapitated head, indicating the trajectory of the sun in its celestial course, is of course an allegorical figure which cuts transversally across many traditions. In India it is found in various other transpositions, as in the case of the head

---

29 At Kāmākhyā this subsitution involves coconut milk instead of *madya* (wine), ginger mixed with salt instead of *māṁsa* (meat), toasted chickpeas for *mudrā*, boiled red leaves for *matsya* (fish) and red sandalwood paste rubbed into the body in place of *maithuna* (sexual union). — Mishra 2004

To linger for a moment on the offering of flowers instead of sexual union, it is no accident that Kāma, to reawaken amorous excitement, shoots floral arrows from his bow.

of the titan Namuci, beheaded by Indra, or that of the hero and magician Makha Viṣṇu.[30] In doctrinal terms it refers back to the figure of the priest Dadhyañc and to the Vedic ritual of Pravargya — called *gharma* (heat) or *mahāvīra* (great hero) — which allows the head cut off as a sacrifice to be restored.

The same Ekavīra — which as we have seen, is one of the names of Māyārūpa-Ellammā — is known in traditional Vajrayāna contexts as Vajrabhairava, the most terrible aspect of Yamāntaka (the killer of death), the black Yamāntaka without a consort. He therefore appears as a kind of counterpart of Dhūmāvatī — who, following the most classical canons of Tantrism, wears a necklace of severed heads, with bone ornaments around his flanks, and uses a skull-cap (*kapāla*) as a cup. And — still another symbolic convergence — it is precisely to Ekavīra that the *śakti-pīṭha* of Jogulambā at Alampur is dedicated, at the very place where, according to tradition, the *āśrama* of Jamadagni was found, while the name Jogulambā is thought to be a corruption of Joginulā Ammā or Yoginulā Ammā (mother of the Yoginī).

The head of Ekavīra is also enthroned in those temples — such as the Saṅkaṭa-Mocana in Varanasi (*fig*. 34) — where exorcism rituals are practised; this goes to confirm the close association of this aspect of the cult with the more tenebrous phenomena of possession.[31]

Parallel to the cult of Ellammā there has also developed another cult venerating the headless body of Reṇukā — *Mātṛrūpa* (maternal form) (*fig*. 35) — which is adored under the name of Bhūdevī or, in certain cases, of Chinnamastā,[32]

30 On this subject see the essay by Coomaraswamy 1944.

31 We cannot escape the similarity between Ekavīra and Rāhu (eclipse), both represented by a head without a body, and both linked with the phenomena of possession and madness.

32 In this particular *mūrti* a flower is generally shown in place of the head, which takes us back to the considerations expressed in the preceding note.

→

and has strong sexual connotations.

Therefore the double recomposition of Reṇukā and the tribal woman, which recalls not only the hot or cold attitudes of the Devī, but also the equivalent operations whereby Māyārūpa was divided from Mātṛrūpa and Rāhu from Ketu, represents the alternation between two poles of the same phenomenon, the often incomprehensible oscillation between sickness and healing. This is connected with the function of the Aśvins, doctors to the gods — another couple, and not by chance — or of the two handmaidens—Yoginīs of Chinnamastā, to whom we shall be returning later.

The dyad of illness–healing is accompanied, in psychological terms, by possession, which can also be read in the light of this double register as either the onset of an alteration in the level of consciousness — hence the possibility of making contact with a chthonic world inhabited by the obscure presences which govern such phenomena — or as the power of salvation of the Devī who enters into the adept's body, making it her temple in view of his final liberation.[33]

The contiguity between the Goddess and possession is

← The cult of the headless Goddess, often represented with her legs apart and her vagina clearly visible, has its roots in the archaic fertility cults of ancient India. Like the snake, which is also linked with fertility cults, in Tantric language she may represent knowledge, as suggested by her appellations Bhūdevī or Bhūmidevī, the earth which must be retrieved by Varāha from the ocean floor (a metaphor for secret teachings) and Chinnamastā, which similarly alludes to an esoteric level of knowledge, by an allegorical transposition which in the West was used (albeit in a less markedly sexual key) by the group of poets known as the *Fedeli d'amore*.

33 Precisely because of this "sacralization" in case of death of those who have contracted a disease, the corpse is not cremated but rather buried or abandoned in water, since it is a vessel of the Goddess.

confirmed by her "menstruating" nature in so far as this condition corresponds to a temporary state of alteration or otherness.[34] Furthermore, the menstruating and therefore impure nature of the Goddess constitutes a reference to the figure of Mātaṅgī and the darker practices of sexual union in the rituals of the left-hand path. This "darkness" of hers emphasizes the absence of that light which, in contrast, signifies generative power, a power precluded during a woman's menstrual period. And this generative incapacity includes a strong symbolic valency because it shifts the Goddess from a function of manifestation to one of non-manifestation, hence of going beyond illusory production. In other words birth, by starting the flow of time, carries with it the inevitability of death, so that the menstruating Devī who prevents the flow of worlds becomes the very image of Mahākāla or of Yamāntaka (the destroyer of death).

---

34 This is reflected in the canonical three days of the menstrual period during which the woman finds herself on the margins of her habitual human nature, almost as if she had shifted to the status of a *yakṣiṇī*, a *nāginī* or an *apsaras*, given that she is considered not only impure, but also dangerous to men and crops, to the extent that she must be segregated.

The three days of the menstrual period hark back to the three days in which the *gandharva* stole and kept hidden from the gods their *soma* (drink of immortality), thereby rendering them mortal and hence themselves potential objects of sacrifice. These are the three days of the new moon which culminate in *amāvasyā*, the dark nights in which Soma, the moon, is kidnapped by the sun. — Filippi 1999

8

Yoginī and Sacrifice

SACRIFICES are offered to the Goddess or to the many aspects under which She manifests — as emphasized by the names of certain terrifying emanations, such as Garbhabhakṣī (foetus eater), or Śiśughnī (she who kills children) — which are capable either of placating her or, according to an equivalent interpretation, of exchanging one life (the victim's) for another (that of the sick person, of the village in which an epidemic has broken out, or the community beset by famine). Hence sacrifice becomes the means for overcoming the apparent ambiguity of the Devī, the instrument available to humankind with which to close the abyss between a universe built on the illusory continuity of time and space, and the void which opens between death and successive rebirth.

This is the long labour to which the Vedic world submitted, erecting the complex edifice of ritual with painstaking thoroughness. But in the last period of the current cycle, in the darkness and haste of the Kaliyuga, human beings lack the qualities to travel such a path at the right pace. And therefore everything is rewritten so that this enormous gap can be closed in one single, incredible leap. So matter, the very structure of the cosmos, transforms itself from a heavy weight to be dissipated in the rarefaction of ritual, into the solid ground on which the practitioner must face up to himself on his journey towards *mokṣa*. A journey which, in the inevitably symbolic perspective of Tantra, tends to manifest by degrees, almost always grouped in numerical series of seven or eight elements.

In fact, there are seven stars in the constellation of the Bear (*saptarṣi*), seven Pleiades (*saptarṣi-patnī*) and seven rivers in the sky (*saptasindhu*). Sūrya has seven horses, seven rays, seven red sisters.

The cosmic egg has seven shells, each one representing a period in the manifestation of the world. There have been seven Manus up to the present *manvantara*, with a further seven to come to complete the Śvetavarāha *kalpa*. Time advances on seven wheels with seven hubs.

Or again, the wood washed up on the coasts of Puri — the body of Kṛṣṇa — was cut into seven pieces.

There are seven illnesses, seven water nymphs — called *sāt saheliāṅ* in the valleys of the Ganges and the Indus, *saptakannigai* in the Tamil regions, *sāt āsara* in Maharashtra — and the children of Cānd Saudāgar poisoned by the snakes of Manasā were seven in number.

And from a Tantric perspective, there are seven principal *śaktipīṭhas*, seven Yoginīs linked with the *cakras* and seven *dhātus*, (constituent parts) of the human body.

At times, but with equivalent symbolic meaning, the numerical series have eight elements. Then they refer to the intermediate world, a world of subtle knowledge and initiatory arts, a world governed by beings appointed to be dispensers of *siddhi*, guardians of the threshold, psychopomps.

These would seem to be functions of the Yoginīs, who are often eight in number, whether as adepts during the rituals of Kaula-*mārga*, as subtle beings in the form of Yakṣiṇīs, as Yoginī-planets or as Yoginīs connected with *śrīcakra*.

But there are also eight paths making up the eightfold noble paths, eight *dharmapālas* (guardians of the law), eight spokes to the wheel underlying the *dharma* itself.

And there are eight *śmaśāna* around Devīkuṭa, the same

number as the *mahāśmaśāna* of the Vajrayāna tradition, and eight sacred *pīṭhas* corresponding to the eight petals of the lotus flower.

In alchemical Tantrism there are eight metals, and *mahāsiddhis* (great powers) are eight in number.

And then the number of Yoginīs who emerged from the body of the Devī is sixty-four, the exponential expression of eight, just as there are sixty-four petals in the *khecarī cakra*, sixty-four Tantra, sixty-four arts of love, sixty-four *siddhis* and sixty-four magic steps leading up to the gate of heaven, according to *Aitareya Brāhmaṇa*.

There have been numerous shifts and exchanges between the two numerical series, like that regarding the number of Mātr̥kā, either Saptamātr̥kā or Aṣṭamātr̥kā according to the myth, or the number of immortals, *ciranjīvin*, seven in the canonical list (Vyāsa, Bali, Vibhīṣaṇa, Hanumān, Aśvatthāmā, Paraśurāma and Kr̥pācārya) but eight if Mārkaṇḍeya[1] is added, or again, in the number of Yoginī-graha, which varies depending on whether or not the group includes Śāntaka, who represents the subtle part of the Rāhu–Ketu duo.

In practice the seven-part series seem to refer mostly to time and the flow of cycles, finding expression in Kālī, the Mahāvidyā who is indeed the consort of Kāla (time). In contrast, the eight-part series assume a spatial connotation, a projection which lies between the human world and the Absolute, a space on which another Mahāvidyā, Bhuvaneśvarī, sets his seal.

We find ourselves in the presence of a typically Tantric view,

---

1 It is significant that at least two of these seven immortals are explicitly connected with places which represent the centre of the world, the base of the world axis: Aśvatthāmā with Badrinātha and Paraśurāma with Paraśurāmakuṇḍa. And this is the same *axis-liṅga* which Mārkaṇḍeya grasped in order to escape from Yama (death) thereby becoming the eighth *ciranjīvin*.

relying on the structure of the manifest world characterized by space and time which becomes a support, a ladder climbed by the *sādhaka* in order to exhaust all its possibilities and finally to transcend it.

But to bring such an ascent to completion, to succeed in going beyond the last step, an extreme leap is necessary, a transposition which once again takes the form of a sacrifice — a sacrifice which, although rooted in Vedic ritual, expresses the atrocity of this dark age, a bloody offering pregnant with magic and recondite meanings, a gesture clinging to the primordial force of the Mother Goddess in her fury of childbirth and dissolution. In this way the red line of sacrifice, which permeates and connects all the divine functions in a feminine key — and it is in this guise that we have always seen the Yoginīs — comes inevitably to colour the esotericism of the Mahāvidyā.

Among them Chinnamastā, who cut off her own head to satisfy the hunger of her handmaidens, evokes this in the most explicit terms, being always depicted holding her severed head while three streams of blood spurt from her neck (*fig*. 36). The nourishment offered by Chinnamastā, those fountains of blood drunk by Jayā and Vijayā (victory and punishment) — elsewhere unambiguously identified as Ḍākinī and Varṇinī[2] — find immediate symbolic equivalents in the *nāḍī iḍā* and *piṅgalā*, while the central *nāḍī*, *suṣumṇā*, corresponds to the spurt which flows back on to the severed head of the Goddess. From another point of view the streams of blood are the three *guṇas* (constitutive qualities), so that Varṇinī is *tamas*, Ḍākinī *rajas* and Chinnamastā *sattva*. Or again, they refer back to the severing of the three heads of the Vedic Viśvarūpa (cosmic form) — the son

---

[2] If the name Ḍākinī is itself a direct reference to the Yoginī, the name of Chinnamastā's other handmaiden, Varṇinī (the coloured one), is also of great interest, since the term is habitually used to indicate members of tribes excluded from the Indian caste system, which leads us back to the figure of Mātaṅgī. — Ramasso 2010

of the creator *asura* Tvaṣṭṛ — by means of which he fed himself, observed the world and read the Veda.[3] Each of the heads cut off by Indra represents in transposed terms a *granthi*, a knot on the practitioner's path to perfection that is untied by Chinnamastā through the destruction of the universe (Viśvarupa), which is none other than illusion (Māyā), and therefore through the sacrifice of the Goddess herself. A function which returns in the removal of obstacles effected by both Gaṇeśa and Ketu, once again divinities who are (re)generated by means of beheading.[4]

It is precisely for this reason that in Tantric settings Chinnamastā is assimilated with Mariyāmman-Reṇukā[5] with whom she shares the power to heal, as well as decapitation.

But her iconography suggests an even more profound message by showing that her beheading has opened the *sahasrāra cakra*, revealing the luminous essence of the Devī and the rising to the surface of *amṛta-soma*, the nectar of knowledge and immortality which had been hidden inside Her. In this way Chinnamastā removes the false perception of duality by freeing

---

3 All these functions are directly linked with Chinnamastā, who feeds Jayā and Vijayā, sees the world with her eye of knowledge, and is a receptacle for knowledge-*soma*.

An equivalent beheading is performed by Indra who, again using *vajra*, cuts off the head of Ṛṣi Dadhyañc for having revealed the teaching of *madhu-vidyā*, thereby "feeding" the Aśvins, the pair of solar twins whose function corresponds, as we shall see, to that of the two handmaidens of Chinnamastā.

4 The functional equivalence with Gaṇeśa becomes even more obvious if we consider that the God is presented with two consorts called Ṛddhi and Siddhi, where Ṛddhi (elsewhere explicitly named Buddhi, Vedāntic term denoting higher intellect) corresponds to knowledge, while Siddhi indicates perfection.

5 One of the best-known cases of this overlapping of cults between Chinnamastā and Reṇukā is that of Vasiṣṭha Gaṇapati Muni, a disciple of Ramaṇa Maharṣi who was deeply devoted to both divinities.

suṣumṇā, which had been blocked at the level of the navel by her very presence.[6]

So decapitation becomes the supreme ritual act, the perfect sacrifice, which taps into the highest knowledge and makes possible the flow of *soma* which takes the adept to full realization. This symbolism is found again in the myth of Durgā Mahiṣāsuramardinī where — in the version recounted in Aruṇācala-Māhātmya of *Skanda Purāṇa* — a *jyotirliṅga* (*fig.* 37) emerges from the decapitated body of the demon-buffalo Mahiṣa, since here the buffalo is an āsuric form of Śiva who, thanks to the intervention of the Goddess, can manifest his divine essence.[7] And yet again in the gushing of the same vital juice of *soma* from the neck of the dragon Vṛtra when it was beheaded by Indra, as told in *Śatapatha Brāhmaṇa*.

Moreover the ritual of Pravargya — the replacement of the head cut off during the sacrifice — is considered *soma*:

> [. . .] because Soma is all things and Pravargya is all things and verily Soma brims over for whoever is capable of understanding this . . . and verily whoever teaches or drinks part of this Pravargya, gains access to that Life and that Light.[8]

All of this is reflected in the reawakening of *kuṇḍalinī* alluded to in the iconography of Chinnamastā, shown seated or standing on the divine couple Kāmadeva–Rati united in their hierogamic embrace, to signify the overcoming of the bonds of cyclic death and regeneration.

In Vajrayāna settings, on the other hand, she takes the

---

6 Here again we recognize the dual function of Devī, who on the one hand blocks and on the other frees the flow of sacred knowledge. The evidence that this happens at the level of the navel has symbolic implications which can be transposed to the sacred geography of Assam, to which we shall return later.

7 Filippi 1993.

8 *Ṛgveda*, translation taken from Coomaraswamy 1944.

name of Chinnamuṇḍā (*fig.* 38), an aspect of the supreme Devī Vajrayoginī, and in this guise she is depicted above Kālī to show her victory over time. This suggests the shift in perspective between the Hindu view, in which she embodies Advaita (non-duality), and the Buddhist view where she alludes to transcendent emptiness.

Therefore she is Paraḍākinī, the supreme Ḍākinī, she who grants the highest *siddhi* and who incarnates the very power of Śakti.

To get drunk on sacrificial blood sipped from the *kapāla*, to gorge on the blood spurting from severed heads or to suck it from the wounds of demons almost as if it were ambrosia (*amṛta*), seems then to be an explicit trait shared by diverse manifestations of the Goddess — whether they be Yoginīs, Mātṛkās or Mahāvidyās — a trait which recalls the quest for the elixir of immortality, a universal metaphor for knowledge.

The allusion acquires further depth in the subtle correspondence between Daśamahāvidyā and Daśāvatāra which, according to *Muṇḍamālā Tantra*,[9] links Chinnamastā herself with Paraśurāma, the *avatāra* who incarnates the destructive power of sacrifice, who is capable of killing all the kṣatriyas, and also of sacrificing his own mother by chopping her head off with a blow from his axe.

The pairing of knowledge with sacrifice emerges very clearly in the dual function of Paraśurāma. He is in fact a master of *śrīvidyā*, the master who, in *Tripurārahasya*, receives the supreme teaching directly from Dattātreya and transmits it to his disciple Haritāyana, who will in turn pass it on to the Sage Nārada so that he can perpetuate the secret doctrine among men. Hence it is in the transmission of knowledge that the close link between

---

[9] *Muṇḍamālā Tantra* (literally the Tantra of the necklace of severed heads) is a text which contains, among others, descriptions of rituals and *mantras* peculiar to Daśamahāvidyā.

Paraśurāma and the cult of the Goddess materializes — a connection transposed into initiatory terms in the beheading and subsequent rebirth of Reṇukā.

Moreover Bhairava, the sacrificer par excellence, on a par with Paraśurāma and like him regarded as an emanation of the god in question — in this case Śiva — is placed in the centre of the circle of Yoginīs to emphasize the centrality of sacrifice in the setting of this cult. So Bhairava comes to represent, at the symbolic level, the centre of the cosmic axis — a terrestrial centre in the case of human Yoginīs, a celestial centre in the case of divine Yoginīs. In this perspective, then, the Yoginīs connected with supports for meditation such as *cakra* and *yantra* articulate, step by step, the practitioner's chance to rise from one centre to the other, by themselves defining that axis.

But the sacrifice (*yajña*) of the woman-Goddess reverberates above all in the origin of the *śaktipīṭha*s, to the extent that it makes them *yajñodakadeśaḥ*s (lands of sacrifice).

Here it is the body of Satī, cut up into fifty-one pieces, which falls to earth becoming the first principle of generation (*fig.* 39). And that the distribution of the Goddess throughout the world is indeed a generative principle is confirmed in the view in which Brahmā, through the three powers of Śakti — desire (*icchā*), knowledge (*jñāna*) and action (*kriyā*) — manifests the entire universe, positioning within it the fifty-one letters called the Mātṛkās, or little mothers, which make it possible to give names and hence form to the world. They are fifty-one in number, like the skulls in Kālī's necklace as she dances on the corpse of Śiva, yet another movement of dissolution and regeneration (*fig.* 40).

This cosmogonic ritual interweaves the universal sacrifice organized by Dakṣa, the sacrifice-incineration of Kāma and above all, the sacrifice of Satī, whose dismemberment gave rise to the *śaktipīṭha*, the sacred alphabet scattered over the earth to reveal to humankind the secret of the Goddess.

Kāmākhyā, which represents the *yoni* of Devī — hence a part for the whole — is the most sacred of the places where the Goddess grants the highest *siddhi* through rituals involving bloody offerings (*fig.* 41). And more than any other temple in India, Kāmākhyā seems indissolubly bound to sacrifice. Here, in fact, apart from minor offerings of sheep and poultry which succeed one another throughout the day, both within the main enclosure and on the altars to other Mahāvidyās which are scattered over the hill, every morning at the opening of the temple a goat is sacrificed, and its blood is sprinkled over the *yoni* of the Goddess. Here during Durgā-Pūjā they celebrate the ritual killing of the buffalo,[10] the animal which, along with *mithuna*,[11] represents the supreme substitute for Puruṣamedha, (human sacrifice), which was widely practised at Kāmākhyā for centuries.[12]

But sacrifice is also associated with this temple on the occasion of other festivities, in which darker Goddess cults emerge which seem to shift from an understanding of Her as a

---

10 As evidence of the non-Brāhmanic setting of these cults, the severed head of the buffalo is carried into the temple and placed at the foot of the altar bearing an iconic form of the Goddess, in the centre of the *mahā-maṇḍapa* preceding the descent into the *garbhagṛha*, as recorded during the VAIS mission of 2010.

11 In tribal settings the replacement of human victims with *mithuna* is rendered even more obvious by the fixing of bovine horns to human skulls, as practised in the villages of the Nāgā, a people found in the southern part of Assam whose name coincides, rather significantly, with that of snakes (*nāga*). — Zanderigo 2002

12 The last human sacrifice recorded by a witness occurred in Kāmākhyā in 1832. The most shocking session of sacrifices, however, dates back to 1565, when on the occasion of the reconstruction of the temple, 140 human victims were immolated, to placate not only Kāmākhyā in her role as Devī of the *yoni* of Satī, but also Kāmākhyā the Lady of the cemeteries, of snakes and of the tribal spirits. — Edward Gait 1906.

generative matrix — symbolized by the *yoni* — to other aspects tending towards dissolution. These cults have their roots in the function of Kāmākhyā (*fig.* 42) as Lady of the spirits and spectres which are to be adored in the *śmaśāna* — evidence for the earlier existence in the territory of Kāmarūpa of a form of devotion tending towards spirit worship and the powers of the left-hand path (*fig.* 43).

The mysteric character of such cults is echoed in the Rājārājeśvarī-Pūjā, a secret ritual dedicated to adoration of the Goddess which is accessible only to Vāmācāra practitioners. This lasts fifteen nights, beginning with the night of *amāvasyā* in the month of Caitra (March–April), and is held in the temple of Kāmeśvara on the hill of Kāmākhyā — that same Kāmeśvara (Lord of Kāma) who lies in sexual embrace beneath the Goddess, and from whom She draws her transformative energy.[13]

Kāmākhyā's inclination towards magical and tribal practices is further confirmed by the myth of Naraka (which is also a name for the underworld) which tells how the Goddess was adored in the land of Kirāta, a mountain people given to the consumption of meat and wine.[14] *Yoginī Tantra,* on the other hand, refers to *kirāta dharma,* a form of devotion followed by the Kirāta in the *yoginī-pīṭha* of Kāmarūpa (the temple of Kāmākhyā). And *Kālikā Purāṇa* describes a practice called *śavara* — the *Śabara,* being an ancient tribal population of the mountains — involving sexual

---

13 Mishra 2004. It is not of secondary importance that reference to Kāma transversally permeates both a series of divine functions (Kāmākhyā, Kāmeśvara, Kāmeśvarī) and the territory of Assam itself (Kāmarūpa).

14 Ramasso 2010. According to *Mānavadharma Śāstra,* the Kirātas were originally kṣatriyas who were downgraded to the role of śūdras for having failed in the duties imposed by their caste. This recalls findings recorded in Odisha among certain tribal communities settled in the forests along the Mahānadī River. — Beggiora 2009.

union with prostitutes, in a power ritual typical of the left-hand path.[15]

And finally, it is Svāmī Karapātrī himself — the most authoritative interpreter of Hindu orthodoxy during the last century — who tells us that Kāmākhyā is linked with knowledge of the *mantra śabara*, the wild *mantra*, which is made up of potent sounds having magic powers.[16]

15 Traditionally, priests destined for the temple of Jagannātha at Puri are chosen from the Śavara (or Saora) of Odisha.

16 Daniélou 1964.

9

Odisha and Assam
Goddesses, Horses and Hidden Knowledge

THE cult of the Yoginī, so widespread in medieval times and so well suited to the Tantric view of the sacred feminine, seems to have lost popularity from the fifteenth century onwards, replaced by devotional practices addressed to other forms of Devī. And yet there is a good deal of evidence of its survival, above all in the more peripheral regions of the subcontinent. The most significant evidence comes from Odisha and Assam, particularly from the area around the temple of Kāmākhyā, where even now the names of the sixty-four Yoginīs are still invoked everyday.

Odisha and Assam — along with certain areas in the south of India — seem in fact to have maintained some continuity of the traditional complex under examination here, bound by a reciprocal connection of which traces can be found in numerous medieval literary sources.[1] This common matrix can be explained by the flowering in these regions of Tantric thought of the so-called Eastern tradition, which branched out into diverse doctrinal streams which influenced and permeated Śākta, Śaiva and Vaiṣṇava cults — particularly those centred on Paraśurāma and Jagannātha — before flowing into Jainism and also Mahāyāna and Vajrayāna Buddhism (although nowadays

---

[1] References to the relationship between Odisha and Assam are found particularly in the biography of the Assamese saint Śaṅkaradeva, in *Kālikā Purāṇa* and in *Burañji*, a corpus of historical literature from medieval Assam.

the last of these have practically been forgotten in Odisha and southern India).

The contiguity of the figure of Jagannātha with the Tantric cult of the Goddess is evident in *Bata Abakṣa* — ascribed to the saint Balarāma Dāsa, who lived in Odisha between the fifteenth and sixteenth centuries — where the God is said to have sixty-four Yoginīs as his attendants.[2] In the classic version of the myth of Jagannātha, the God Kṛṣṇa appeared to Indradyumna in a dream, asking the king to make an image of him (*mūrti*) from a tree trunk that would wash up on the beach at Purī the following day; this tale explains the origin of the three *mūrti* housed in the temple of Purī in Odisha. In a variation of the myth taken from *Yoginī Tantra*, Kṛṣṇa ordered the king of Kaliṅga to use an axe (and here the use of a *paraśu* recalls a sacrificial gesture) to cut the tree trunk from the sea not into three but into seven pieces.[3] Later the king would send two of these pieces to Kāmarūpa, where they would be carved into images of Hayagrīva and Mādhava (or Matsya) to be installed in the temple at Hajo.[4]

So the variation of the myth found in *Yoginī Tantra* seems to posit a "consubstantiality" of the *mūrti* venerated at Puri with

---

2 Rath 2009.

3 The symbolic structure of wood-sacrificial body-principle of manifestation echoes the theme of Prajāpati, in which the universal progenitor is beheaded and divided — or else divides himself — "[. . .] like a tree whose top is split . . .", or even more explicitly, the question "Which wood and which tree were used to fashion heaven and earth?" (*Ṛgveda* X.31.7) and the response "*Brahman* is the wood, *Brahman* the tree".

4 Hajo, ancient capital of the Assamese kingdom of Ahom, was central to the world of Tantric schools in north-eastern India. In the area of Hajo, apart from the temple of Hayagrīva, there are the hill of Kāmākhyā and Vasiṣṭha-Kuṇḍa on whose banks, according to tradition, stood the hermitage of Vasiṣṭha. And Hajo is the place where *Mahābhārata* locates the retreat of the Pāṇḍavas during the last year of their exile.

that in Assam. And there is further evidence for the relation between Jagannātha and Kāmarūpa in the deep roots of his cult in the Assam area, not to mention the singular coincidence whereby the name Nīlācala (blue mountain) designates both the place where the temple of Jagannātha stands at Purī and the hill of Kāmākhyā.[5]

---

[5] By a curious coincidence, these two temples had a similar fate, both being destroyed in the first half of the sixteenth century by the iconoclastic sovereign Kālāpahāṛ after his conversion to Islam.

Even more significant is the correspondence between the place name Nīlācala and the name of a type of blue stone at the heart of a complex of Odishan tribal myths documented by Stefano Beggiora during research trips to Saora areas.

A first myth tells of a Saora hunter named Basu (Viśvabasu or Basuśavara, depending on the version) who in the depths of the jungle secretly adored the God Jagannātha in the form of a statue made of blue stone. King Indradyumna, sovereign of Mālvā, sent four brāhmaṇas to the four points of the compass in search of Viṣṇu. One of them, Vidyāpati, went deep into the forest and came upon the house of the Saora hunter. Basu made him welcome, and once the brāhmaṇa had won his confidence, led him to the secret location of the image of Jagannātha. The God, after thanking Basu for his years of devotion, said he was tired of that place and wanted new and better sacrifices. He was ready, in fact, to leave the blue stone to become Jagannātha, Lord of the World. On hearing these words the brāhmaṇa rushed back to his king, but when they both returned to the secret place, the image was no longer to be found. From the skies above a divine voice announced that only after the sovereign had practised 100 Aśvamedhas, the God would manifest in the form of a trunk of wood, to be recognized by certain signs. So Indradyumna performed the sacrifices and the trunk appeared; after having it fetched, the king called the best sculptors and smiths of the realm to give the wood the form of the divinity of blue stone.

Another version depicts Indradyumna in a more sinister light. Having learned that the blue stone was in the forest, the sovereign wanted at all costs to remove it and make its power his own. To →

However, although Odisha and Assam both play major roles in the sacred geography of India thanks to the diverse currents of Tantrism, Assam (Kāmarūpa or Prāgjyotiṣa) — which once included the areas of modern Arunachal Pradesh, Nāgāland, Meghalaya and Tripura — seems to present a more subterranean character, in which the mysteric connotations of Yoginīs and Daśamahāvidyā prevail over the exterior manifestations dear to popular devotion such as Kālī, Durgā and Saptamātṛkā.

There are in fact many texts confirming the importance of the cult of the Yoginīs in this region. *Kaulajñāna Nirṇaya*, for example, affirms that the Yoginī Kaula doctrine has spread to every household in Kāmarūpa. And *Yoginī Tantra* offers an even clearer indication by emphasizing that, while each of the *pīṭha* is particularly sacred in a particular period, Kāmarūpa has this distinction in the current Kali-Yuga.

But Kāmarūpa, apart from its literal meaning of "form-desire" (the world where forms are born of desire), in the

---

← punish the king's pride, Jagannātha disappeared, but after the intercession of Basu, the God agreed to the transfer on condition that 100 Aśvamedhas be offered to him. In the end the king obtained the image of the God, but Jagannātha never appeared to him personally.

The replacement of the rough-hewn blue stone by a trunk of wood carved by a carpenter — Viṣṇu symbolizes the transition from a tribal cult practised in the darkness of the forest to a grand solar cult. But there is also a certain affinity between the *mūrti*, or sculpted image, and the wooden idols traditionally adored by the Saora in their sites in the jungle.

In a setting traditionally remote from this, we find connections with the story *Della ricca ambasceria la quale fece lo Presto Giovanni al nobile Imperadore Federigo*, which is part of the collection called *Il Novellino — Le ciento novelle antike*. Here the Stonecutter of "Prester John, the very noble Indian Lord" was sent to the court of Federico II to reclaim the gift of the three stones "of great virtue", whose powers the emperor had not understood and which therefore had to be removed from his empire.

sandhyā bhāṣā idiom of the *siddha* coincides symbolically with a downward-pointing triangle; so from this perspective, all of Assam represents the *yoni* of the Goddess, a *yoni* which therefore becomes the centre of India, which in turn — like all traditional kingdoms — is an expression of the entire world. And in the heart of Kāmarūpa stands Kāmākhyā, the most important of the fifty-one *śakti-pīṭha*, which even today is still a point of reference for the Dakṣiṇācāra and Vāmācāra paths of the Devī cult. And finally, inside the temple, sunk deep inside its *garbhagṛha* in the form of bare rock, lies the *yoni* of Satī which fell on earth.

This concentric concatenation, which culminates in the place where a fall — hence a descent — of divine influence took place, is recognizable as a traditional description of the centre of the world, itself an emanation or reflection of the supreme spiritual centre. And the same centrality is acknowledged in Vajrayāna contexts too, since in *Hevajra Tantra*,[6] Kāmākhyā is indicated as one of the four sacred centres of Tantric Buddhism.

Furthermore, it is on the northern borders of Assam, not far from Kāmākhyā, that Vajrayāna tradition localizes Pemako (unfolding, *ko*, of the lotus, *pema* or *padma*),[7] the most important of those secret places (*beyul*) which, according to Tantric Buddhist doctrine, make special paths to liberation accessible to those who are qualified. They represent points of discontinuity in the flow of illusory manifestation, hidden lands where several

---

6 *Hevajra Tantra* is a *Yoginī Tantra* composed in north-eastern India (probably in Bengal) between the ninth and tenth centuries. It takes the form of a dialogue between Bhagavān Buddha and his disciple Vajragarbha and also includes dialogues between the God and his consort. *Hevajra Tantra* was one of the first Tantric texts to become widely known in Tibet.

7 In Hindu and Buddhist spheres, the lotus is regarded as a metaphor for the awakening of the mind. For this reason divinities — and in certain cases the platforms of the temples which house them — rest on lotus flowers which symbolize their enlightened essence.

levels of the individual being may be realized simultaneously, freed from the bonds of contingency.[8]

In addition to this possibility of transposition, which makes the *beyul* equivalent to the *tīrtha*, in the case of Pemako we are faced with a form of sacred geography on which is projected the body of the Goddess Vajravārāhī (in Tibetan Dorje Pagmo) (*fig.* 44), queen of all the Ḍākinī and a visualization of the knowledge which is able to break the chains of becoming. She constitutes one of the most esoteric expressions of the supreme Devī and again presents many of the peculiarities of Kāmākhyā but from a Vajrayāna perspective. Here, however, the function of the Goddess is explicated in mysteric terms because, although the various *cakra*s of Vajravārāhī (Dorje Pagmo) have been ritually opened over time thanks to the revelations of specific *ter-mā* (treasures hidden in the form of texts or mantric instruments of power), the uterus (*yoni*), called *chimé yang-sang-né* — immortal secret inner place — which according to doctrine constitutes the paradisiac region hidden at the innermost point of the Pemako *beyul*, is still secret, only to be unveiled at the end of this cycle of time (*pralaya*).[9] This part of the Goddess's body, which slopes down towards the plains of Assam, is known as "the secret forest of the Ḍākinī", opening out in mountains and jungles concealing magical medicinal plants. Here the Devī takes the name of Dorje Pagmo Ludrolma, Vajravārāhī in the form of a snake charmer, thus offering further evidence in a Buddhist key

---

8 The same places can at times become the scene of fleeting experiences devoid of awareness, for those who have not developed an appropriate level of consciousness. This is the case of people who, after accidentally crossing a subtle threshold, enter environments where time passes at a different speed, or those who glimpse, at the bottom of a lake, a city in which a parallel life is unfolding. These are fantastic events whose narrative structure is found in the sagas of many countries, such as — to take an example close to home — the legends of the Monti Pallidi in the Dolomites.

9 Baker 2004.

of the close relation between medicine, poison, transformation and the reawakening of *kuṇḍalinī*.

The *neyig*, texts which provide information about the secret lands, describe the *yang-sang-né* of Pemako as surrounded by eight cemeteries and identify it, in brief, as the subtle place at the centre of the eight *mahāśmaśāna* Vajrayāna, making this *beyul* a reflection of Sambala, an ultramundane kingdom equivalent to Brahmapura, the celestial centre of Hindu tradition. By extension, the whole of Pemako is therefore considered to be the greatest of the cemeteries, the preferred dwelling place of the Ḍākinī, the *śmaśāna* in which *yogin* and *yoginī* visualize themselves being ritually dismembered by an emanation of Dorje Pagmo.[10]

And then Pemako, like Kāmākhyā and Paraśurāma Kuṇḍa, is situated at the eastern gateway of the territory to which it traditionally refers, in this case Tibet, alluding symbolically to the shrinking back to the original state of manifestation which takes place at the end of a cosmic temporal cycle — an original state marked by the watery presence of the Tsangpo/Brahmaputra, which here flows southwards in a large curve before precipitating into the plain of Assam, a further metaphor for the event which gave rise to the universe through the liberation of the waters.[11]

---

10 Meditation on the dismemberment and stripping of the flesh from one's body by the Goddess, and consequent visualization of one's own skeleton, is one of the Tantric techniques of the Chod Vajrayāna. This technique is echoed in the tribal context in the ecstatic dreams of shamans, during which they witness the beheading and dismemberment of their bodies by spirits or demons.

11 The cosmogonic myth of Indra's liberation of the waters held back by Vr̥tra contains numerous elements pertinent to this study. Vr̥tra in fact has the form of a huge snake (a reference to the titans, gods in the previous era and to the *sarpa-vidyā*), and the weapon used by the king of the gods to behead him is a *vajra* (which is connected →

Also linked to the Tantric Buddhist world is the Vaiṣṇava temple of Hayagrīva on the hill of Maṇikūṭa, the site of ancient Hajo (Assam). The two traditions share not only this hypostasis of the god, who plays an important role in both, but also the hill itself, which under the name of Tsam-cho-dum (rTsa-mchg-gron), is considered to be the sacred *stūpa* of the Buddha's *samādhi*.

Kālikā Purāṇa relates that Maṇikūṭa was the very place where Hayagrīva killed the fever demon Jvarāsura, consort of Śītalā, thereby enacting the victory of the light of knowledge over the darkness of death. But in yet another reversal, in the same text Hayagrīva is also the demon who guards the eastern gate of the kingdom of Prāgjyotiṣapur (the ancient name for Assam) of king Narakāsura, who in turn is linked with the myth of Goddess Kāmākhyā.

Moreover Hayagrīva, along with Yamāntaka — the destroyer of death whose relation with Ekavīra-Reṇukā has already been mentioned — is one of the eight *dharmapāla*s, terrifying guardians of the *dharma*[12] who, as Guénon reminds us, are equivalent to the eight paths of the Eightfold Noble Path, the eight petals of the "lotus of the good law" or the eight spokes of the wheel which represent the *dharma* itself.[13]

A tradition of Tibetan origin holds that on the cliff of Neta Dhubunir Pat Sil, near Tsam-cho-dum (the temple of Hayagrīva), the Buddha entered into *parinirvāṇa* and was cremated. This place is the Sītāvana *śmaśāna* (Sil-wa-tsal-gi-dur-khrod or

← with the middle way and hence with *śrīvidyā*). The fall of the waters alludes to the rain, and thus to the descent of knowledge. And it should not be forgotten that this view has a direct microcosmic correspondence in human birth, which occurs after the "breaking of the waters".

12 Bianchi 2006.

13 Guénon 1946. Here we cannot escape a reference to the Yoginīs who, as we have seen, are identified with the rays/petals of the *maṇḍala*.

"pyre of fresh earth"), the first of the eight *mahāśmaśāna* (great cemeteries) of the Vajrayāna tradition — the *śmaśāna* of the east, the one where Padmasambhava himself experienced initiatory death, being devoured by a Ḍākinī and then travelling through her *cakra* as far as the most secret lotus, the supreme place of burial. So the Ḍākinī-Yoginīs are the subtle vehicles allowing those who are qualified — as in the case of Padmasambhava — to reach *sahasrāra*, the last *cakra* of the human body, the supreme lotus at the crown of the head, beyond which all links with manifestation are severed, and one arrives at the state of *jīvanmukta*. Furthermore Padmasambhava, as the initiator of the Vajrayāna tradition, represents a descent of the divine principle, so the indication that it was here that He reached supreme liberation, the premise to carrying out his mandate, symbolically makes this place the earthly centre of the cosmic axis.

Again, in the area around Gauhati we find the temple of Ugra-Tārā, one of the Daśamahāvidyā whose cult is common to both Hindu and Buddhist Tantric circles, but which has had a particular doctrinal and devotional development in the Vajrayāna sphere. *Nīla Tantra*[14] describes the Goddess in the centre of four flaming funeral pyres, with a *muṇḍa-mālā* around her neck, a tiger skin around her hips and a corpse as her *vāhana*. She is the powerful vibration which breaks through primordial immobility.

---

14 *Nīla Tantra* or *Bṛhad Nīla Tantra* is a text of the Kaula school which describes the Goddess as one of the three aspects of Tārā (Eka Jaṭā, Ugra-Tārā and Nīla-Sarasvatī), specifically Nīla-Sarasvatī, the sapphire blue Sarasvatī, *śakti* of the divinity in her creative aspect linked with knowledge. In this aspect She is also the Goddess of the fifty-one letters of the alphabet. The thirteenth chapter of the text describes the *vīra sādhanā* of Mahākālī — the way of the hero, which involves sexual practices — along with the principles of *svecchācara*, the path of individual will, which is one of the central practices of the Kaula school.

The Sage Vasiṣṭha was a devotee of Tārā and a follower of Cīnācāra — a spiritual path described by medieval Tantric authors as rooted in the region north of the Himalaya — and it was to him that Viṣṇu, in the aspect of Buddha, revealed the secrets of *pañca-makāra*.[15] One of the traditional versions of the life of this great *ṛṣi* locates his hermitage on the banks of the Vasiṣṭha-Kuṇḍa (*fig.* 45), near Hajo, interweaving his myth with those of Naraka and of Kāmākhyā. And Vasiṣṭha-Kuṇḍa itself, the sacred pool fed by three springs, represents a powerful *tīrtha* able to guarantee — according to *Kālikā Purāṇa* — the attainment of the supreme Heaven to those who immerse themselves in it.

However the two most important places for ritual ablutions in Assam — Brahma-Kuṇḍa and Paraśurāma-Kuṇḍa — are located even further to the east, in the farthest reaches of Bhārata. Brahma-Kuṇḍa is the sacred shore where after a long penitence, Paraśurāma finished his expiation for the sin of matricide and was rewarded by the axe (*paraśu*) detaching itself from his hands.[16] Finally the God hurled it into the distance, where it fell and lodged at a bend in the Brahmaputra, at the very point where the riverbed leaves the mountains to enter the plain of Assam — a place known ever since then as Paraśurāma-Kuṇḍa (*fig.* 46).

---

15 Ramasso 2010.

16 Here an analogy emerges with the skull-cap (*kapāla*) of the fifth head of Brahmā which fell into the hand of Bhairava once the guilt of Brāhmanicide had been expiated. However, to dwell on the relation between the severed head and *paraśu* would be superfluous. It seems more important to emphasize how the completion of atonement, hence reintegration into the state of perfection, takes place in the case of Bhairava in Benares at a site known as Kapāla-Mocana (the liberation of the skull), an ancient *kuṇḍa* which is considered to have been the most important *śmaśāna* (cremation ground) in Varanasi in an earlier age. Evidently we are once again in the presence of a *tīrtha*, a point where it is possibile to pass beyond the cyclic nature of time, a function which by extension, is traditionally assigned to the entire city of Kāśī (Benares).

At a symbolic level these two *tīrtha*s seem particularly meaningful, as transpositions of the two phases of the reintegration of the individual into the Absolute. From this perspective Brahma-Kuṇḍa corresponds to purification, a return to the state of the state of real manhood (*vīra*) or in Western initiatory terms to the lesser mysteries, whereas Paraśurāma-Kuṇḍa, characterized by the *paraśu* — which like the *vajra* is an axial symbol and at the same time an instrument of sacrifice[17] — is the place where one can transcend the self to arrive at the state of transcendental man (*divya*) hence the path of greater mysteries.

Although distinct in their functions, the two *tīrtha*s coincide geographically and therefore constitute — reasoning in axial terms — the projection on to the same point of two different possibilities. This view is confirmed by evidence collected during the VAIS research missions of 2008 and 2010 from Hari Bābā (*fig.* 47), the brāhmaṇa appointed to preside ritually over Paraśurāma-Kuṇḍa.[18] According to this authoritative source, the *tīrtha* represents not so much a gateway leading beyond *pralaya* — a function traditionally performed by the temple of Jagannātha at Purī — as a point located beyond the manifest world. It therefore constitutes, for those who recognize it as such and possess the qualifications, reintegration into the axis connecting the terrestrial with the celestial pole in a prospect of non-return, hence of ultimate liberation (*mokṣa*).[19]

---

17 The *paraśu*, like *vajra*, finds a correspondence in the two-headed axe or more generally in two-edged weapons. — Guénon, 1962

18 Interviews recorded in the course of the VAIS research missions of March–April 2008 and November 2010 in Assam and Arunachal Pradesh, coordinated by Gian Giuseppe Filippi.

19 According to Hari Bābā an equal value is accorded to Badrinātha and Jośīmaṭha, two places sacred to Śaiva Tantrism which are perched among the mountains in the far north of India.

It is interesting that Jośīmaṭha is also one of the four *maṭha*s of the →

Furthermore, both these *tīrtha*s are found in the same place as the cave where Paraśurāma (*fig.* 48) withdrew or hid, thereby becoming the only *avatāra* not to have been reabsorbed into the transcendent Viṣṇu. Among these descents of Viṣṇu — all characterized by an evident sacrificial function — he who is the incarnation of the supreme sacrificer has not in fact completed his mandate, since he has not yet transmitted to Kalkin (the last *avatāra*) the knowledge of the art of destruction which will render Kalkin capable of starting the *pralaya*.

According to the Tantric view which posits a subtle relation between Daśamahāvidyā and Daśāvatāra, Kalkin corresponds to Tripurasundarī, the Goddess immanent in the three worlds, pure knowledge (*śrīvidyā*). Thus knowledge becomes a synonym for liberation: liberation from the universal cycle in a macrocosmic perspective, liberation from the cycle of death and rebirth in a microcosmic perspective.

So here, elements which foreshadow the supreme Centre reappear in a Vaiṣṇava key — just as they did at Kāmākhyā with a Śākta function. The presence in a cave — a place which is the epitome of that which is hidden or withdrawn — of Paraśurāma in "inactive" mode while waiting for another descent, Kalkin, to manifest and then precipitate at the same point, therefore

---

← Śaṅkarācārya placed at the four cardinal points of India, specifically that of the north. The eastern point is found at Purī, coinciding with the temple dedicated to Jagannātha whose *mūrtis*, as we have seen, was made from the same wood. Kṛṣṇa sent to Hajo to make the images of Hayagrīva and Matsya, the two "polar" functions of the cycle of Viṣṇu. This translation therefore reflects in symbolic terms the shift of the centre of Vaiṣṇava Tantric tradition from Odisha to Assam, in preparation for the *pralaya*.

There is evidence of a similar perspective in the title *jagadguru* (universal master) proper to the Śaṅkarācārya, while Jagannātha — with a similar title — represents the celestial projection as "Lord of the universe".

confirms the function of Paraśurāma-Kuṇḍa as the terrestrial pole of the cosmic axis.

As we have seen, there are numerous references to secret or hidden places which in various ways imply the presence in Assam of a traditional centre which has withdrawn from human sight. The identification of Kāmarūpa as a hiding place is found also in *Mahābhārata*, which locates the refuge of the Pāṇḍavas during the last period of their exile in the kingdom of Matsya in the area around Hajo.[20]

The story of Pāṇḍavas again connects with this territory at a point on the northern bank of the Brahmaputra, near Gauhati, where the horse of Arjuna's Aśvamedha is thought to have bathed during his ritual voyage retracing the orbit of the sun. And the same northern bank is indicated by tradition as the dwelling of Yoginī with terrible powers.

The theme of the horse recurs not far away at Aśvakrānta (*fig.* 49), again on the north bank of the Brahmaputra, which *Yoginī Tantra* considers to be the greatest of the *tīrtha*, more powerful than Puṣkaraṇa (Puṣkar, Rajasthan) or even Gaṅgā (*fig.* 50). The myth, which is still very much alive in Assamese tradition,[21]

---

20 The symbolism of hiding in the forest is found again in Odisha where, near Bhubanesvar, there is another important *tīrtha* concealed in the forest where Rāma was exiled. But this hiding place in Odisha relates to Rāma, hence to a period earlier than that of the Pāṇḍava who are linked with the story of Kṛṣṇa, the subsequent *avatāra* of Viṣṇu — which goes to confirm the shift of the traditional Vaiṣṇava centre from Orissa to Assam.

21 The entire myth of Naraka (or Narakāsura) — presented in different versions in *Kālikā Purāṇa*, *Harivaṁśa* and *Yoginī Tantra* — provides abundant references and evidence of the special role of Assam in the Tantric doctrinal ambit.

Naraka in fact is the son of Bhūmi (the earth mother Goddess) and Viṣṇu in the form of Varāha; already this genealogy indicates a double ancestry, both Brāhmanic and tribal (in this regard see n 32 →

tells how Kṛṣṇa stopped here to water his army's horses before

← of Chap. 7 on the overlapping between Bhūmi Devī and *Mātṛ-rūpa* Yellammā and Reṇukā), while here Varāha offers a clear suggestion of the theme of hidden knowledge. The child was found in King Janaka's cremation ground, with his head resting on a skull poking out of the earth. After being rescued and taken to the court, Naraka was raised by the king as an adopted son. It was only at the age of sixteen, with the help of Bhūmi Devī, that he discovered the identity of his real father, Viṣṇu, and resolved to leave the court of Janaka.

Later, with the assistance of Viṣṇu, Naraka wrested the kingdom of Prāgjyotiṣa from the Kirāta king Ghaṭakāsura and became its sovereign (Prāgjyotiṣa in this sense becomes the projection on earth of the celestial kingdom), on condition that he offer his exclusive devotion to the pre-existing divinity Kāmākhyā. One day, after years of good government, the Goddess appeared to Naraka, who fell in love with her but was rejected with a trick: after promising to yield to him if he were able to build a temple in her honour in a single night, when the construction was almost complete Kāmākhyā brought forward the cock crow, bringing the night to a premature end. Consequently Naraka's devotion to Kāmākhyā dwindled, and he abandoned himself to demonic influences (*asuraṁ bhavamvadya*) which manifested as a kind of possession, inevitably leading the king to ruin and death, beheaded by his own father (in the guise of Kṛṣṇa).

Janaka, Naraka's adoptive father, reappears in other legends as sovereign of the kingdom of Videha in southern Nepal (see n 3, Chap. 7), a sovereign extremely well versed in religious doctrine — and particularly in the śrīvidyā — to the extent that in *Tripurārahasya*, he is given the part of the sage king who imparts one of the principal teachings in the text to a brāhmaṇa.

This complex web of stories confirms the strong bond between the Vaiṣṇava tradition and Kāmākhyā — the only divinity to whom even a son of Viṣṇu owes his devotion — as well as the alternation between *eros* and *thanatos* in the relationship with the Goddess, an alternation which the *vīra*-practitioner must learn to keep in the right perspective, lest he be completely ruined. The dual nature, divine and āsuric, of Naraka is also of great symbolic importance, along with the fact that he receives from Janaka an education (evidently →

crossing the river and killing King Naraka (*fig.* 51) — sovereign of that same kingdom whose eastern gateway was guarded by the demon Hayagrīva — and placing his son Bhagīratha on the throne of Prāgjyotiṣa.[22]

Aśvakrānta is a particularly important site in the Kṛṣṇaite ambit because it was here that the God stopped to rest with his armies after kidnapping his future bride Rohiṇī (Rukmiṇī), the daughter of Bhīṣmaka, during the wedding procession organized by the *asura* Śiśupāla, the bridegroom who had been imposed on her. In this Assamese version, the myth holds that Rukmiṇī was born in a village close to Paraśurāma-Kuṇḍa, namely Bhīṣmakanagar in the district of Lohit (Arunachal Pradesh).[23]

← of a doctrinal nature) so elevated that at the age of sixteen, the age of transition, he is capable of recognizing and identifying with his own divine nature.

Finally, the ancient skull on which the child Naraka was found resting inevitably brings to mind Golgotha (the place of the skull), which in Christian tradition represents the skull of Adam, found at the base of the hill on which will be raised the cross of Christ (the new Adam), who through his sacrifice will make possible the reopening of the path towards heaven. All this is an evident representation in a Western key of the symbolism of the cosmic axis (the cross) with its two terrestrial and celestial poles, where the terrestrial pole is symbolized, as in the case of Naraka, by a skull cap — which is none other than the vault of the chthonic world on which the new Adam stands to bring order to the world.

22 The mention of the name of Bhagīratha recalls the myth of Gaṅgāvataraṇa and constitutes a symbolic reference to the revival of knowledge by means of the descent or liberation of the waters. On the function of Bhagīratha in the primordial descent of the Gaṅga, see Zanderigo 2009.

23 The myth confirms the importance in Vaiṣṇava circles of the area of Paraśurāma-Kuṇḍa which in this circumstance is identified with the kingdom of Vidarbha. And the very name of Rukmiṇī, →

Furthermore, Aśvakrānta is also the name of a collection of sixty-four Tantras belonging to the Śāktāgama corpus, which is traditionally subdivided into three parts relating to geographical zones. It represents — and this is no accident — the northern part extending from the Vindhya chain of mountains as far as Tibet, which reinforces an interpretation of these places in terms of sacred geography.[24]

Therefore the horse, a creature of water, remains symbolically linked with the *tīrtha* and, like the rain which suggests the descent of celestial influence — equivalent to the descent of knowledge — also functions as an agent of the dissemination of knowledge from the sky to the earth.

And the horse's function of connecting the two poles of the cosmic axis also recurs — necessarily — but acting in the opposite direction, in one of the most important sacrificial rituals of the Vedic world, the Aśvamedha, or sacrifice of the horse (*fig.* 52). This culminates with the ascent of the animal's spirit — a substitute for the *cakravartin* — along the *aśvattha* (the sacrificial pole symbolizing the polar axis), allowing the sovereign to go beyond the heaven of the fixed stars, and identifying him as Transcendental Man. The ritual encapsulates certain elements

---

← who although she is *āryā* is also called Rohiṇī (the red), and of the husband who was imposed on her, the *asura* Śiśupāla (child eater), recalls a tribal setting. Finally it is worth stressing that in astrological terms, Śiśupāla also represents the southern pole star corresponding to the eye in the constellation of Taurus.

This version of the myth was received from the brāhmaṇa of the temple of Aśvakrānta during the VAIS research mission of November 2010 to Assam and Arunachal Pradesh, which was coordinated by Gian Giuseppe Filippi.

24 The same tripartition is also found in *Sammoha Tantra*, although here the texts relating to the north take the name of Cīna, since it was the Cīnācāra school which, according to tradition, was brought to Assam by the Sage Vasiṣṭha. — Rao 2005

typical of the Tantric tradition, elements which are particularly evident in the sexual union under a cloth of the queen with the corpse of the horse — a union which must take place on the night of *amāvasyā*. Here we find the function of psychopomp exercised by the woman–goddess–*prakṛti*, and the themes of the uterus-cavern as a place of death and regeneration, of the night which covers the sky like a curtain and symbolizes the moments of cessation or annulment in the cycles of manifestation, and of the awakening of *kuṇḍalinī* from *mūlādhāra cakra* to make its ascent along the *merudaṇḍa*.[25]

Moreover, the horse sacrificed in the Aśvamedha has its mythical origin in a horse which emerged from the ocean and was first greeted as a gift of Yama, and later assimilated to the God himself and to the sun. And the association of this animal with Yama is found again in another sacrifice in which it is the God of death himself who acts as officiant, being rewarded with the offering of a horse.[26]

Again, the sacrificial horse is called "Lord of Hosts" (Gaṇānāṁ Gaṇapati), originally an epithet of Bṛhaspati and of Indra, but subsequently attributed to Gaṇeśa, a God connected with the transmission of initiatory knowledge, who was himself beheaded and whose head was replaced by that of an elephant.[27]

This view recurs in another passage from *Śatapatha Brāhmaṇa*

---

25 The Aśvamedha suggests many other trains of thought which are significant for the present study. Here we will do no more than recall that it is celebrated after the recognition of a *cakravartin* (a universal sovereign, literally "he who makes the wheel turn") who, during the Vājapeya ritual, climbs to the top of a pole to which is attached a wheel — representing the zodiac belt — and leans out over it, since he is now capable of seeing beyond the circle of fixed stars.

26 *Śatapatha Brāhmaṇa* IV.3.4.27 and 31. For a deeper analysis, see Malamoud 2002.

27 Coomaraswamy 1944.

which affirms that the Aśvamedha is the moon herself, a metaphor for the Goddess or for the cup of *soma* (elixir of knowledge and immortality). And to confirm the function of the horse in the transmission of knowledge, it should suffice that Kalkin (*fig.* 53), characterized by his white charger, and Hayagrīva horse-headed god (*fig.* 54) are linked with the withdrawal and the restitution of the Veda from one cycle to the next.

Finally, the trio of horse–Devī–knowledge finds an explicit echo in the Vajrayāna setting where the sound issuing from the throat of Dorje Pagmo is compared with the neighing of Hayagrīva, embodying the language of the knowledge of all the *buddhas*.

Around this symbolic identity revolves the entire mythical apparatus of Dadhyañc, the *ṛṣi* to whom Indra revealed two secret doctrines, forbidding him to divulge them on pain of beheading. Dadhyañc, however, transmitted them to the Aśvins (solar twins) whence they were handed down to mankind in secret teachings passed from master to disciple. These primal doctrines are the *pravargya-vidyā* — that is the science of how to install a new head on to a body beheaded during sacrifice — and the *madhu-vidyā* (science of honey), a sublime form of knowledge which leads to liberation.[28] However, the Aśvins found a way to elude Indra's prohibition by first using the *pravargya-vidyā* to behead the *ṛṣi* and replace his head with that of a horse. In this new equine form, Dadhyañc transmitted to them the higher teaching — the *madhu-vidyā* — and when Indra then inflicted on him the punishment of beheading, as announced, the Aśvins went to get the *guru's* original head and placed it back on his neck.

As well as reaffirming the horse's role as a vehicle for the transmission of knowledge, the Vedic myth therefore constitutes a point of reference for sacrifice by beheading and for recovery

---

28 Filippi 1996.

or substitution of the head, anticipating what will be developed in the later myth of Reṇukā.

The story also has a sequel which is equally crucial for our purposes. Once his mortal life was over, Dadhyañc retired to the skies, and from that moment on āsuric forces took command of the earth. Indra, worried, searched for the *ṛṣi* without success, and after learning of his departure, decided to recover a part of his body to use as a weapon to defeat the enemies of the gods. He found the horse's head which was lying hidden, awaiting the end of time, on the bed of Lake Saryaṇavat on the plain of Kuru (where the final battle of Mahābhārata would later take place) — or according to another version, in a lake on Mount Saryaṇavat[29] — and using the jaw bone, was able to exterminate the ninety-nine Vṛtras.[30]

---

29 Doniger O' Flaherty 1975.

30 The myth shows noteworthy parallels with that of Samson, the twelfth judge of Israel. He is a singular figure who eludes the classic canons of mercy and justice of Biblical heroes, as demonstrated by the episode in which after losing a wager, "[. . .] the Spirit of the Lord came upon him, and he went down to Ashkelon, and slew thirty men of them, and took their spoil, and gave the garments to those who had solved the riddle. . . ." (Judges 14: 19).

He seems therefore to embody the role of sacrificer, where sacrifice is far from being a ritual oblation, corresponding rather to the inscrutable fury of the divine (the spirit of the Lord came upon him) — a fury of destruction and regeneration — following a logic which does not belong to the Jewish world. Here we have a gratuitous oblation, an annihilation performed by a sacrificer who, in the end, goes so far as to sacrifice himself. Therefore the figure of Samson would seem to conceal an archaic element, a reminder — albeit incomplete — of a different traditional order.

As for the convergence with the Indian myth, Samson, like Indra, uses the jaw bone of an animal — in this case of an ass, not a horse (and this is not the place to enlarge on the symbolic significance of the two animals) — as a weapon to exterminate 1,000 Philistines. →

This recalls Varāha, who immersed himself in the primordial

← This is the most bloodthirsty of the acts of the Biblical hero, and the thousand Philistines, like the ninety-nine Vr̥tra massacred by Indra, represent the indeterminate multitude, almost an entire category which is exterminated, as in the case of the kṣatriya wiped out by Paraśurāma. After he had thrown his weapon down at a place known as Ramat-Lechi (jawbone hill), in the throes of a mighty thirst (the burning sun as a vehicle of death), Samson invoked the Lord, who satisfied him by creating a hole in the slopes of the hill from which a spring of water gushed. So the well on the hill of Ramat-Lechi recalls the theme of the mountain lake where the jawbone of Dadhyañc lies.

Furthermore, if Indra is the god of the solar dynasty par excellence, in Hebrew Samson means sun while Delilah, his wife, contains the root of the word for "night" (*laylah*). But as we have just seen, rather than a sun dispensing life, he is rather the midday sun, the sun which parches and incinerates, the sun of the sacrificial fire.

Like Manu, who is the son of an "identical woman", a mirror image of the true wife of Vivaśvat (the sun), Samson also has a miraculous genealogy, having been conceived through divine intervention by a barren woman whose husband is called Manoach, a name which may be recognized as a corruption of Manu. And his birth is announced by a divine Messenger who then returns to the heavens, ascending with the flames of the sacrifice offered by Manoach.

But perhaps the most significant point is the passage where he challenges the guests invited by his future bride to solve a riddle: "Out of the eater came forth food, out of the strong came forth sweetness." (Judges 14: 14). The answer, given within the required seven days and obtained through trickery (as the Aśvins used trickery to elude Indra's punishment and obtain knowledge), is this: "What is sweeter than honey? And what is stronger than the lion?" Here we may find a parallel with the gushing of *amr̥ta* from the beheaded body of Chinnamastā (out of the eater came forth food), and also with the dual knowledge of Dadhyañc: *madhu-vidyā* and *pravargya-vidyā*. And this last will be used by Samson once his head has been shaven (beheading) to make his hair grow again (the sun's rays) and reacquire the powers of the sun-lion ("what is stronger) (than the lion?") to carry out the final destruction.

ocean to rescue Bhūmi Devī, the earth, a metaphor for hidden knowledge. But the myth also offers a series of references which together provide a concise summary of the characteristics of Paraśurāma and Kalkin, the two Vaiṣṇava avatāras who preside over the final dissolution and who stand at the centre of the axial symbolism of Paraśurāma-Kuṇḍa.[31] Thus the two lakes or *tīrthas* where the horse's head is hidden — one in Kurukṣetra, the place which determines the end of the Dvāpara-Yuga and hence the beginning of the subsequent Kali-Yuga, and the other on a mountain peak (a symbolic substitute for the cave) — are once again reflections of the Supreme Centre where the weapon is hidden (or the equivalent master of weapons, Paraśurāma) which will lead to the *pralaya*.[32] This unusual instrument of death — a substitute for the *vajra* (thunderbolt), which is Indra's usual weapon — is nothing less than knowledge itself, which is able to overcome the apparent end of the universe, defeating death. And the correspondence should be noted between the teaching about sacrifice with subsequent substitution of the head — which perfects a ritual that would otherwise be ineffective — and initiatory death and rebirth of knowledge.

Yet all of this turns out to be mere preparation, the narrow

---

31 The link between Dadhyañc and Paraśurāma — and hence Reṇukā, who obviously shares the same function — is confirmed by his belonging to the lineage of the Bhārgava — descendants of the great R̥si Br̥gu — an ancestry that he has in common with Jamadagni and Paraśurāma.

32 It is worth mentioning that this image finds a correspondence in the Western tradition in the sword Excalibur of the Arthurian cycle, another two-edged weapon hidden in a lake and guarded by the Lady of the Lake, a being who in all aspects resembles a Yakṣiṇī. This theme preserves symbolic elements having a universal character in its identification of lake, water, basin and uterus, elements found in an even more explicit form in the tree of *śamī* — which as we have seen is comparable to a mother's womb — among whose branches the Pāṇḍavas hid their weapons.

doorway we must pass through to reach the real ambrosia offered by Dadhyañc, *madhu-vidyā*, the science of honey, the final teaching capable of revealing the path towards *mokṣa*. Here the Tantric symbolism of the cup made from a skull-cap is revealed — a cup which contains knowledge itself in the form of the elixir of immortality. This is the aim of the ritual, this is the recondite meaning of the *kapāla* exhibited by the Yoginīs.

A similar vision reverberates in the function of the Aśvins (*fig*. 55), the doctors to the gods who embody the thaumaturgic powers of Āyurveda — hence again, the power over life and death — who are characterized precisely by honey and a horse's head. The Vedic divinity Soma is also considered capable of healing, and in this sense *soma-vidyā*, the science of which the Aśvins are masters, is equivalent to *madhu-vidyā*.

Even more significant is the relation between the Aśvins and the *nāḍīs iḍā* and *piṅgalā*, which correspond to the two rivers Gaṅgā and Yamunā, while Sarasvatī/*suṣumṇā* represents a synthesis of the twins or in other terms, Dadhyañc himself, who after his beheading "feeds" the Aśvins with the nectar-knowledge of *madhu-vidyā*. Here we have a recurrence of the symbolic structure encountered in the iconography of Chinnamastā, the Mahāvidyā who sacrificed herself to satisfy the hunger of her handmaidens — Yoginī, Jayā and Vijayā. In that case, too, the beheading guaranteed free flow in the three *nāḍīs*, which is equivalent to the emergence of *amr̥ta-soma*, the food of immortality which unseals the rebirth of knowledge.

If in this sense the Aśvins are reflected in Chinnamastā, there is much further evidence of their contiguity with the potency of *śakti*, traces of which can already be found in *R̥gveda*.[33] This contiguity becomes explicit in the invocation in *R̥gveda* VII.67.5: "Grant us a strong spirit in battle and protect us with your *śakti*, O Lords of Śakti".

---

33 *R̥gveda* I.34.8, II.39.5-6-7, VI.63.5, VII.67.5 and VII.68.3.

Thus the function of the Aśvins shifts to a more subtle terrain, a terrain where the power exercised over illness-healing is sublimated in the potency which brings to life the alchemical knowledge of the Āyurveda and alludes to the transmutation of the body into an instrument of realization. For this reason they are called Māyāna or Lords of *māyā* (illusion), one of the epithets of the Goddess, or those who attain Śrī, well-being — another reminder of the Devī and of *soma* — through Śacī, a feminine word clearly associated with *śakti* which in *R̥gveda* indicates the powers of the gods.

And it is precisely in this mastery of them over the powers of *yoga* — a mastery highlighted by *manas* (mind), their charioteer, a metaphor for the alchemical body[34] — that the Aśvins suggest, from the Vedic period onwards, that traditional complex which later merged with the *siddha* and the Tantric schools of medieval times.

The same significance recurs in their essential nature as twins, a mark of the doubleness which is articulated in complementarity or synthesis, as testified by other pairs which replicate the same symbolism on different planes. Thus the Aśvins are the two eyes whose sight is transfused into the third eye, the eye of knowledge, also called *bindu*. They are *udāna-vāyu* and *apāna-vāyu*, the upward and downward winds which merge in *samāna-vāyu*, the calm state of breathing and of the mind known as yogic *samādhi*. They are Yamunā and Gaṅgā which flow into the subterranean River Sarasvatī. They are Skanda and Gaṇeśa whose origin is Śiva himself. They are the *r̥ṣis* Agastya and Vasiṣṭha, Chinnamastā's handmaidens Ḍākinī and Varṇinī, Gaṇeśa's consorts R̥ddhī and Siddhī, the divine brothers Balarāma and Kr̥ṣṇa. They are Agni (fire) and Soma

34 *R̥gveda*VII.69.2. *Manas*, represented by a stalk of sugar cane (*ikṣudaṇḍa*), is also one of the attributes of Goddess Tripurasundarī, which therefore harks back to the same doctrinal order.

(moon), or again Mitra (sun) and Varuṇa (waters)[35] which in union as Mitra–Varuṇa represent the supreme state of *yoga*, also known as *soma-loka*, *satya-loka*, *sahasrāra cakra* or the thousand-petalled lotus, realm of immortality.

The myth of Dadhyañc finds a curious echo in that of the *asura*s Madhu and Kaiṭabha who stole the Vedas, hiding them at the bottom of the ocean. Viṣṇu, in the form of Hayagrīva (his horse-headed hypostasis) intervened to defeat the two demons and rescue the Vedas. Apart from the allusive names of Madhu and Kaiṭabha — meaning respectively honey and bee larva, hence referring to the *madhu-vidyā*, as has been clarified by Gian Giuseppe Filippi[36] — the myth seems significant because of the concealment of the Vedas on the ocean floor, a clear reference to the *vajra*-horse's head hidden in Lake Saryaṇavat, which posits the symbolic equivalence of *soma*-sacrificial beheading with *vajra*-knowledge, in this case represented by the Vedas.[37]

If subtle or hidden knowledge is connected with the Devī and the Yoginīs, the place name Devīkoṭa, Devīkoṭṭa or Devīkūṭa (village of the Devī), a mythical place hidden on the borders of

---

35 Agni, Mitra, *piṅgalā*, sun and fire are associated with the masculine principle and the *maṇipūra cakra* located above the navel, whereas Soma, Varuṇa, *iḍā*, moon and water are associated with the feminine principle and the *svādhiṣṭhāna cakra* at the level of the navel. The latter location, in microcosmic terms, recalls Chinnamastā and relates to what will be said shortly on the correspondence between the *śakti-pīṭha* and certain traditional centres in Assam.

36 Filippi 1996.

37 A further symbolic equivalence may be discerned with the myth of Gaṅgāvataraṇa, the descent to earth of the Ganges, which is introduced by an episode in which the horse to be sacrificed in course of the Aśvamedha organized by King Sagara (Ocean) is stolen by Indra and hidden on the dry bed of the ocean, at the bottom of *pātālaloka* beside the hermitage of Kapila. Later Sagara's nephew, Suman, who represents right intention (*śraddhā*), was charged with recovering the horse. For further details, see Flippi 2009.

Assam,[38] also seems to refer to such knowledge. *Devīrahasya*[39] includes Devīkūṭa among the eight sacred places corresponding to the eight petals (Bhairavas) of the lotus. In this case the other petals are Kāmarūpa (Kāmākhyā), Malaya, Kaulagiri (the hill of the Kaula), Cauhara, Kulāntaka, Jalandhara and Oḍḍiyāna. In a similar perspective the diverse *pīṭha* are identified with the Devī presiding over them, and here Mahālakṣmī — a synonym for Tripurasundarī — is assigned to Devīkoṭa.

Virūpa, a great *mahāsiddha* of the Vajrayāna school who lived in the seventh to eighth century, known as the "master of the Ḍākinī", performed some of his miracles at Devīkoṭṭa, a hermitage hidden deep in the forests between Bengal and Odisha.

Devīkūṭa recurs in *Kālikā Purāṇa* as one of the seven *pīṭhas* of the Devī along with Uḍḍiyāna — birthplace of Padmasambhava — which some sources identify with Orissa, Jalandhara (the *mahāmokṣa-dvāra* or "doorway of the great liberation" situated in the Goddess's throat),[40] Pūrṇagiri, Kāmagiri (Kāmākhyā) and

---

38 The name Devīkūṭa offers another interesting reference because *kūṭa* (or *khaṇḍa*) are the parts into which the *pañcadaśī mantra* of the Srīvidyā school is subdivided, parts which are symbolically related to the head, shoulders and hips of the Goddess. This last part is called Śaktikūṭa or, precisely, Devīkūṭa and like the innermost and most sacred part of Pemako, encloses within itself the womb of the Goddess.

39 *Devīrahasya Tantra* (*Tantra of the Secret of the Devī*) — also known as *Dakṣiṇamūrti Saṁhitā* — is a technical text dealing almost exclusively with *mantra, yantra, pūjā* and *sādhanā* referring to different aspects of the Goddess.

40 It is no accident that Jalandhara is also the name of an *asura* king born of the meeting between a ray of light from Śiva's third eye and the ocean. He uses Rāhu, the eclipse, to send Śiva a request that the Goddess Pārvatī be given to him alone. In this myth too, an interweaving of many of the allegorical figures we have already encountered is evident.

two further *pīṭhas* described as lying on the borders of Kāmarūpa on to which fell the Devī's head — perhaps a reference to the head of Reṇukā which rolled far from her body, coming to rest in an area of untouchable Śabara — and her navel.

Here the seven *pīṭhas* recall the seven *cakras* of the Goddess's body, and it is interesting that as many as three of them are concentrated in Assam, with a further two probably found in Odisha. Elsewhere Uḍḍiyāna — or Oḍḍiyāna — seems to allude not so much to a geographical place name as to the land of the Oḍiyyā, shamans and Yoginīs endowed with great powers and dark knowledge, which goes to emphasize the interchangeability, in symbolic terms, of Yoginīs and *cakras*.[41]

Finally, of the two *pīṭha-cakras* on the borders of Kāmarūpa, one might be found in the tribal area among the foothills of Arunachal, where Ākāśī Gaṅgā is held by local tradition to be the head of the Devī; significantly, it lies just at the opening of the valley which leads to Pemako.[42] The site of the *śakti-pīṭha* corresponding to the navel remains to be identified, although the same text locates it somewhere in the eastern part of Assam. But in the light of what has already been said about the function of Paraśurāma as master of the doctrine of the Devī and consequently first cause or navel of knowledge, along with his analogy with Chinnamastā–Reṇukā, who at a microcosmic level is in fact placed at the navel, it does not seem imprudent to link this *śakti-pīṭha* with the *tīrtha* of Paraśurāma-Kuṇḍa at the easternmost point of Assam. However, the same equivalences recur with an opposite meaning inasmuch as, in *Abhidhānottara*

---

41 Oḍḍiyāna or Uḍḍiyāna, the birthplace of Padmasambhava, in the Vajrayāna tradition is identified with the mythical kingdom of Sambala, the "pure land" cited in numerous texts including *Kālacakra Tantra*.

42 *Ākāsa* (ether, the highest of the five elements) is the one found inside the heart, at the centre of the human being, another indication of centrality in the sacred geography of Assam.

Tantra,[43] the Goddess Vajrayoginī–Vajravārāhī corresponds to the navel, while Paraśurāma–Reṇukā refers to the severed head of the Goddess, hence to the uncovering of the *sahasrāra cakra*. From this it follows that the two positions are undifferentiated, in that they project the same symbolic significance, whether the point of view is that of Vajrayāna or Hindu Tantra. What remains unchanged is the orientation of the Devī, who presents her *yoni* manifested at Kāmākhyā, on the western border of Assam, stretching out across the whole of Kāmarūpa and extending her head towards the east. So in terms of sacred geography, we come back to what has already been emphasized about the position of the Yoginīs inside the *maṇḍala-cakra*, where they are arranged like the spokes of a wheel, with their feet resting on the circumference — a metaphor for the world of multiplicity — while their heads reach towards a subtle centre — the origin, the unmoved mover of the universe — which alludes to a reabsorption into the primordial centre which here is to be located at the eastern edges of Bhārata.[44]

---

43 *Abhidhānottara Tantra* is a Tantric text of the Vajrayāna Buddhist tradition. It contains two lists, each of which names a series of seven Yoginīs dedicated to initiation (Yāminī, Trāsinī, Anekakāmā, Rūpisañcalā, Bhasurā, Ṭākinī, Kāraṇaṇī and Rūpiokā, Cumbikā, Lāmā, Parāvṛtrā, Sāvalikā, Anivartikā, Ehiki Devī).

44 Then again, returning to the myth of Reṇukā — who we have found to be closely connected with these places — we find a passage which clarifies how after being repudiated by her husband Jamadagni, she travelled to a forest "in the east" to devote herself to *tapas*, thereby confirming the allusion to a wild place in the east where it is possible to return to the primordial state. In the same version we come across a further convergence because during her eastern retreat, two saints appeared to Reṇukā in a dream, and suggested a ritual of expiation so that Jamadagni might take her back. Their names were Ekanātha and, significantly, Jogīnātha. After completing her atonement she returned to her husband and was beheaded. But her head multiplied and scattered in all directions.

These themes reappear and reconnect in a Vajrayāna perspective, in which setting they offer — and it could hardly be otherwise — equivalent symbols and clues to interpretation. So Devīkūṭa, in the sacred geography of Pemako, is the place where the *yoni* of Vajravārāhī/Dorje Pagmo is to be found, the *yang-sang-né*, the most secret point, the last *cakra* of the Goddess which has not yet been revealed. The same Vajravārāhī who embodies the esoteric form of the Devī, a transposition of the secret knowledge which opens the path to realization, the same Vajravārāhī whose consort in the mystic union is Hayagrīva, he who on the one hand gives voice to the language of the wisdom of all the *buddhas*, and on the other acts as a demon guarding the eastern gate of the kingdom of Prāgjyotiṣapur, Assam.

Here the theme of hiding is renewed in the name of Padmasambhava, the master who brought the teachings of Buddhism to Tibet, subjugating all the spirits which infested that country. And in Tibet the great master coupled with three women: Tashi Chidren of the Monpa ethnic group (a people with the role of guardians of the threshold), Dorje-tso and Yeshe Tsogyal — also known as Dechen Gyalmo — a princess of the house of King Karchen. Yeshe Tsogyal was also his disciple and together they concealed *ter-mā* which would reveal secret places (*beyul*) of which Pemako, according to Padmasambhava himself, is the most dangerous and the most extraordinary of all, "a celestial kingdom on earth".[45]

---

45 For the Nyingmāpā school, Yeshe Tsogyal is the most important of the Ḍākinī, an incarnation of the Goddess Tārā. In this guise she is assimilated with Vajravārāhī, mother of the *buddhas* and source of the other Ḍākinīs, "innumerable as the grains of dust making up Mount Meru".

In the Chod ritual the principal deity who acts as a support for meditation is Yeshe Tsogyal herself, who here takes the name of Troma Nakmo, the black Ḍākinī, the Black Mother of the *vajra*. She represents the method revealed by the *siddha* and *ter-ston* →

In the *ter-mā* revealed by Dudrul Dorje and entitled Self-liberation through hearing of the great blissful land of Pemako, Padmasambhava explains the conditions necessary for opening the hidden land:

In a future age, armies will invade Tibet from east and west.

In order to benefit the suffering Tibetans, I, Padmasambhava, have prepared the hidden lands.

Of the many hidden valleys, the most extraordinary is the great blissful Buddha Realm of Pemako.

Just recalling it for only a moment opens the path to Buddhahood.

There is no need to mention the benefit of actually going there . . .

Many kinds of samādhis *will arise spontaneously in one's mind . . .*

The wisdom channels will open . . .

I, Padmasambhava, and an ocean of siddhas *and Ḍākinīs* as *well as peaceful and wrathful deities can all be directly seen . . .*

A miraculous "power grass" grows there; whoever finds and eats this plant, even old men, will become like sixteen-year-old youths . . .

There is a grass called tsakhakun*; whoever eats this grass can have visions of various celestial realms and underworlds.*[46]

According to Khamtrul Rinpoche, there are five supreme magical herbs in the *beyul* Pemako: one which increases happiness, one which bestows immortality, one which makes it possible to fly through the sky like the Ḍākinīs, one which confers all the supreme *siddhi*s and one which reveals intrinsic realization.[47] Once again we are in the presence of substances which evoke

---

← Dudjom Lingpa, of the lineage of Khyeuchung Lotsawa, one of the twenty-five principal disciples of Guru Padmasambhava, who had also revealed the *dharma* to the birds (a further link with the Yoginī–Ḍākinī).

46 Baker 2004: 453.

47 Ibid.: 463.

the power of transformation, a transformation associated with the experience of pilgrimage to these extraordinary places.

And of all the possibile pilgrimages to the *cakra* of Vajravārāhī/Dorje Pagmo, there are three circumambulations (*koras*) winding around the *yang-sang-né*. Here, at the summit of a promontory in the middle of the river Yang Sang, the sacred geography of the Goddess's *yoni* takes the form of four caves corresponding to the four cardinal directions. In the highest cave there are two sacred springs, one of the water of life (*tshe-chu*) and the other of the nectar of life (*tshe-chang*).[48] The four caves are surrounded by eight cemeteries where 725 deities dwell. And crowning this sacred mount, next to the small *gompa* of Devīkoṭa, lies the seat of Padmasambhava, a *ter-mā* revealed by Dudjom Lingpa, in the very place where, according to Guru Rimpoche himself, the new humanity will be regenerated after the *pralaya*.

So if in Odisha references to the Goddess, to Jagannātha and hence to the great theme of man's relationship with the transcendent are made in an explicit fashion, the same references are found in mysteric terms in the easternmost reaches of Kāmarūpa.

In Odisha there are vestiges of temples to the Yoginīs, but it is in Kāmākhyā that they are still adored even today.

Kāmākhyā gives evidence of the Devī in the Kali-Yuga, her *yoni* bathed in blood, the black night of dissolution, the return into the great womb, mouth of death and threshold of liberation through the most secret and extreme Tantric practices.

Hajo is the domain of Hayagrīva, hypostasis of the Kalkin and a *deva* or *asura* according to one's point of view, who is enthroned in a Hindu sanctuary which is also sacred to Vajrayāna Buddhism, made from the same tree trunk which gave substance to Jagannātha. But that trunk is none other than

---

[48] The two springs have a direct symbolic equivalent in Western tradition in the issue of water and blood from Christ's side.

the skeleton of Kṛṣṇa who returns from the flood waters as the god of a new manifestation and hence, if Jagannātha is he who ferries humanity from one cycle to the next, Hayagrīva-Kalkin determines the beginning and end of the cycles.

So if Purī represents the "exterior" seat of Jagannātha, through more veiled hints Kāmarūpa guards his presence in retreat in this extreme moment of the Kali-Yuga.

At Devīkūṭa stands the hidden seat of Padmasambhava who, like Jagannātha, presides over the gateway from one cycle to another, from one humanity to the next.

There lies the great *śmaśāna* of Pemako, the still unrevealed *yoni* of Dorje Pagmo, a projection of Sambala beyond this period of time.

There, at the easternmost extremity of Assam, is the *tīrtha* of Paraśurāma-Kuṇḍa, cut into the mountain to allow the waters to flow in the renewal of the primordial cosmogonic sacrifice.[49]

There lies the cave where Paraśurāma hid to await the *pralaya*, the last act of manifestation.

There is the mountain where the Kalkin will descend to perform the extreme sacrifice.

---

[49] At Cape Comorin, in the far south of India, there is an important *śakti-pīṭha* dedicated to Bhagavatī Kanyākumārī, a sanctuary of particular importance for the Śrīvidyā school. Tradition holds that the *mūrti* was installed there by Paraśurāma himself who, with a stroke of his axe into the sea, reclaimed the land for the temple. Here, as at Paraśurāma-Kuṇḍa, we are in the presence of axe blows into the waters which open and close the sacred land of India.

10

The Triad of Knowledge

THE continuous intertwining of all these elements hint at a complex symbolic scaffolding permeating all of India since archaic times, which filtered into Vedic rituals as much as tribal village cults, and completely infused the medieval Tantric world. This hidden scaffolding holds the keys — technical and ritual — which allow human beings to overcome their eternal longing to reunite with the Absolute, giving meaning and an end to their existence.

But to complete the picture and bring everything back to the theme of this study, to grasp the function of the Yoginīs in the labyrinth of Tantra, a further note is required on that tripartite structure of knowledge which finds its fullest expression in the esoteric doctrines of Devī.

The invocation of the thousand names of the Goddess contains three affirmations which are illuminating in this respect: "You are the embodiment of knowledge. You are the mistress of the Tantra. You are the light in the triangle." The last phrase indicates the triangle as the geometric transposition par excellence of this tripartite symbolism (*fig.* 56).

The *śrīyantra*, the most elevated support for defining all the levels which lead from multiplicity back to the One, is in fact made up of triangles. Diverse combinations of triangles form the *yantra* used by the *sādhaka* in their meditation practices; in the most essential, an upward-pointing triangle intersects a downward-pointing triangle, completed by a point in the middle — a summary in concise terms of the all manifestations and its cause (*fig.* 57).

Two triangles — Traipurā and Kāmakalā — open and close the *merudaṇḍa,* the subtle axis of the human body, a projection in microcosmic terms of the two poles of the cosmic axis (*fig.* 58). At the base of the spinal column the three sides of Traipurā are presided over by the triad of Jyeṣṭhā, Vāmā and Raudrī, personifications of will, knowledge and action. Inside this triangle dwells Tripurasundarī in the form of the *bija mantra 'klīṁ', kuṇḍalinī* coiled around herself before reawakening. And it is precisely the snake-like form of *kuṇḍalinī* — along with the presence of Jyeṣṭhā, explicitly suggesting a link with Śītalā–Manasā — which harks back to the *sarpa-vidyā.* At the other end of the *merudaṇḍa* stands Kāmakalā, the supreme triangle, the dwelling of *śakti* deployed in all her potency, She who is attained through *madhu-vidyā,* She who offers access to the supreme science of *śrīvidyā.*

The highest tripartition of the Devī finds its greatest symbolic transposition in the innermost part of *śrīyantra,* that is in the first triangle enclosing the *bindu* — the central point of the *yantra* and the undifferentiated origin of all manifestations — offering a further series of Tantric triads linked with the cult of the Goddess, who here takes the name Tripurāmbā (mother of the triad) and whose attendants are the *ati-rahasya* Yoginīs (the extremely secret Yoginīs). In a continuous symbolic cross-referencing between the subtle axis of the human body and the different parts of *śrīyantra,* the first triangle, like that at the vertex of *merudaṇḍa,* is called Kāmakalā while its three angles, representing the three forms of power of the mother-goddess, correspond to the triad of Vāmā, Jyeṣṭhā and Raudrī who, as we have seen, preside over the triangle at *mulādhāra cakra.* At the same time these deities are also Kāmeśvarī, Vajreśvarī and Bhagamālinī, whose seats in the sacred land of India are respectively Kāmarūpa-pīṭha (Goddess's left eye), Pūrṇagiri-pīṭha (her right eye) and Jalandhara-pīṭha (the point between her two eyes).

These three seats, along with the fourth, non-manifest seat called Uḍḍiyāna-pīṭha (whose attendants are the *parāpara-rahasya* Yoginī, the Yoginī beyond all secrets), represent in a three-point scale (or from another perspective, in a four-point scale) the centrality of Devī in sacred geography which has already been emphasized in its seven-point form. Here another extremely interesting element emerges because, if Kāmarūpa-pīṭha proves to be the only one whose geographical location is certain (that is, the temple of Kāmākhyā), within the structure of *maṇḍala* it corresponds to the north, whereas Jalandhara-pīṭha is placed in the south and Pūrṇagiri-pīṭha in the east. This spatial reconstruction would therefore confirm the existence of a centre located to the east of Kāmākhyā, a centre referring to the deity Vajreśvarī (Lady of the *vajra*) — and here the overlapping between Vajreśvarī and Vajravārāhī reaffirms the ideas so far expressed about the sacred geography of Assam, and projects the supreme centre and celestial pole of the cosmic axis into the Uḍḍiyāna-pīṭha, the secret land of Yoginī.

The *bindu* itself, in a kind of primal tendency towards symbolic fragmentation, is called *traya* (triple), and alludes to the three deities Kāmeśvara, Kāmeśvarī and Tripurā, whose anthropomorphic expression is made up of the two breasts and the face of the Goddess[1] or — in cosmic terms — of the sun, the moon and the fire of awareness.[2]

Further triads unfold as will (*icchā*), knowledge (*jñāna*) and action (*kriyā*) — the three powers of Śakti — or the epistemological triad of the knower (*jñatṛ*), knowledge (*jñāna*) and the known (*jñeya*) or again, as the three phases of the cosmogonic process, creation (*sṛṣṭi*), preservation (*sthiti*) and reabsorption (*saṁhāra*).

---

1 Precisely these elements (Goddess's breasts and face) emerge in the Svayambhu (born of itself) image in a pothole in the river which bathes the *śakti-pīṭha* of Ākāśī Gaṅgā in Arunachal Pradesh.

2 Schwarz 2009.

And furthermore, Devī is *saccidānanda*, comprehending in herself essence (*sat*), consciousness (*cit*) and bliss (*ānanda*), in which we can find her equivalence with the state of *prajñā* and hence her identification with undifferentiated *ātman*, which is held to be outside and beyond all the particular conditions which determine each of the diverse states of manifestation.[3]

And Kāmākhyā, whose aniconic *mūrti* is lodged in the underground *garbhagṛha* of the temple, is also venerated in three forms: Ṣoḍaśī, Kamalā and Mātaṅgī, three Mahāvidyās who are identified with Lakṣmī, Sarasvatī and Durgā,[4] who in their turn are the Devī-śakti of Viṣṇu, Brahmā and Śiva.[5]

The very name of Tripurasundarī again presents the same metaphor: it is translatable as "goddess of the three cities", and indicates the three diverse paths to salvation, *sarpa-vidyā*, *madhu-vidyā* (or in other words *pravargya-vidyā*) and *śrī-vidyā*, the triad of Tantric science, the three levels through which the practitioner must climb to reach liberation (*mokṣa*).

In an even more significant interpretation, Tripurasundarī (*fig.* 59) is translated as "goddess earlier than the three", that is the one who came first, hence she who transcends the three, where the triads referred to may be the three Vedas, the three sacrificial fires, the three states of consciousness — waking (*jāgarat-sthāna*), sleep (*svapna-sthāna*) and deep sleep (*suṣupta-sthāna*); the three times — past, present and future; the three

---

3 Guénon 1925.

4 In the correspondence with the three Devī-śakti, we may also recognize the three functions of the *saṁnyāsin* — here meaning he who possesses knowledge — namely *bālya* (retracted or embryonic function), *pāṇḍitya* (teaching function) and *mauna* (function of perfection) which also corresponds to *kaivalya* (isolation). Here, in fact, Lakṣmī, Sarasvatī and Durgā are transposed into the three *siddhis* which belong to *jīvanmukta* as a secondary consequence of perfect metaphysical realization. — Guénon 1925

5 Ramasso 2010.

worlds — *bhū* (earth), *bhuva* (atmosphere) and *svaḥ* (sky); the three dynamic qualities (*guṇas*) — *sattva*, *rajas* and *tamas*; or, finally, she who dwells in the three subtle channels (*nāḍīs*) of energy — *iḍā*, *suṣumṇā* and *piṅgalā*.[6]

All these triads connect symbolically with Śiva's trident (*triśūla*), whose shaft (*daṇḍa*) functions as an axis, a fourth subtle element which projects a level of knowledge beyond ordinary awareness.[7] So they constitute a concise synthesis of many of the elements fundamental to Indian thought, which due to their symbolic implications and doctrinal complexity, deserve a separate investigation. Here, however, it is worth dwelling at least on the last triad, the one made up of the three *nāḍīs* — *iḍā*, *suṣumṇā* and *piṅgalā* — to emphasize a few points which are crucial to our purposes (*fig*. 60).

Piṅgalā is development, the growth of the seed, and also the name of one of the five snakes (*nāgas*) to which the celebration of Nāga-Pañcamī is dedicated. Even more allusively, in a myth of which traces can be found in both Hindu and Buddhist literature, it is the name of one of the four snakes which guard the four great hidden treasures — Śaṅkha in Benares, Paduma at Mithila, Piṅgala at Kaliṅga (Odisha) and Elapatra at Taxila — placed in the four cardinal directions among which Piṅgala — not by chance — is the guardian of the east.

Iḍā in turn is the solemn offering, *śraddhā* (faith in the effects of sacrifice), hence the bride of Manu, through whom

6 Pelissero 1995.

7 This symbolic reading of *triśūla* and its handle (*daṇḍa*) recalls one of the most elevated teachings in the metaphysics of Vedānta, the description of the diverse conditions of *ātman* — or four *pāda* — of which the first three appertain to all the possibilities of manifestation, to all the possibilities of non-manifestation, and to the universal possibility, while the fourth, *turīya*, corresponding to the handle, transcends them, indicating the unconditioned state of *ātman*. — Guénon 1925

he generates descendants,[8] and also the remains (*ucchiṣṭa*) of the sacrifice itself.

Some of the synonyms for *suṣumnā* are equally significant, particularly *brahma-nāḍī* (*nāḍī* of Brahmā), *mahāpantha* (great way), *śakti-mārga* (path of the Goddess), *madhya-mārga* (middle way) and, for the reasons given above, *śmaśāna* (cremation ground).[9]

In a macrocosmic perspective *suṣumṇā* corresponds to Mount Meru, the polar axis, which joins the centre of the world with the celestial centre, passing through it to reach beyond the heaven of the fixed stars — as is recalled in the Aśvamedha ritual — or, at the microcosmic level, passing out of the *brahmarandhra*, beyond which identification with the Absolute is realized, hence the attainment of final liberation.

Moreover, if in cosmological terms *iḍā* and *piṅgalā* relate to Sūrya and Candra — the sun and moon — *suṣumṇā* relates to Rāhu or his complement Ketu — the eclipse and the comet — where the eclipse, being the overlapping of the moon and sun, symbolically represents the maximum luminosity, a luminosity so dazzling as to become at the same time the darkest part, the black night of the Yoginī, that same obscurity found inside the heart or the mountain cave. This symbolism is taken up in architecture in the form of the finial placed at the summit of the Buddhist *stūpa*: a series of rings indicating the higher heavens is topped by a sickle moon and a sun disc surmounted by a flame — a flame which is the light of Agni, but also the darkness of the eclipse — pointing out the ultimate path, the gateway leading out of the manifest world.

---

8 Lévi 1898.

9 Eliade 1954.

11

Yoginīs as Shadows of the Middle Path of Śrīvidyā

At this point, with all the elements displayed in front of us, we will take our cue from René Guénon before making the decisive step.

In one of his last works, *The Great Triad,* he emphasizes how the two Tantric paths of the right hand (Dakṣiṇācāra) and the left hand (Vāmācāra) may be regarded as related to the two "outer" *nāḍī*s in the human body — *iḍā* and *piṅgalā* — that are like two snakes coiled around a central pole, symbolically representing the power over life and death, or by analogy, the maternal and the destructive sides of the Devī. Thus *piṅgalā* and *iḍā* refer to *sarpa-vidyā* and *madhu-vidyā,* while the central *nāḍī* — *suṣumṇā* — which passes through the successive *cakra* of the human body and then out of the *brahmarandhra* at the top of the head, is identified with *śrīvidyā,* the Middle Way — in diverse traditions considered the highest path — to which the other two paths become secondary specifications.[1]

It is again Guénon who relates the two Tantric paths to the power of the *vajra,* a symbol formed by two double lateral volutes

---

[1] Evidence that this is a matter of secondary specifications — hence of minor mysteries — is found in the fact that the Vāmācāra *mārga* clearly aims at the attainment of *siddhi,* even independently of the prospect of final liberation. And if the Dakṣiṇācāra *mārga* presents itself as a right-hand path alternative to the Vāmācāra inasmuch as it is ritually pure, this confirms that it acts at the same level.

around a central axis.[2] The *vajra* (diamond or thunderbolt, a synonym for purity and incorruptibility) — *dorje* in Tibetan (*fig.* 61) — is the quintessential Vajrayāna ceremonial instrument. Its ritual complement is the bell (*dilbhu*), representing a circle or cup, which suggests *prajñā-pāramitā* (transcendent knowledge). These two elements — circle/cyclic nature and transcendent knowledge — are two primary prerogatives of Yoginīs, the same two highlighted by Cāmuṇḍā and Vārāhī, and in this regard a connection has already been observed with the two petals of *ājñā cakra*.

The centrality of the *vajra/dorje* in the Tantric Buddhist sphere offers a further cue, if we consider that it is an attribute of Devī — Dorje Pagmo — who is enthroned in the *beyul* of Pemako, the earthly pole of the cosmic axis according to Vajrayāna tradition. The same view is replicated in the Śākta setting, where the terrestrial pole corresponds to Kāmākhyā, and also in the Tantric Vaiṣṇava context, which locates the base of the axis at Paraśurāma-Kuṇḍa.

The only position which would seem to be missing here is the Śaiva, but from the viewpoint of the cyclic nature of time and the worlds, Śiva is transversally present, summing up in himself the function of destruction — or rather, transformation — in a regenerative key. He is in fact the cause of the sacrifice of Satī and of its effect, the emergence of *śakti-pīṭha*. He is Bhairava at the centre of the circle of Yoginīs, He is the Lord of *yoga* and of cemeteries, hence of Pemako, the greatest among them. He is the ten Rudra, counterparts of the Daśamahāvidyā, He is Kāla (time), bridegroom of black (Kālā), He is the great sacrificer who shares the same weapon (*paraśu*) with Paraśurāma. He is akin to Kalkin on the last day of the *pralaya*.

---

2 An equivalent symbolism relating to the power over life and death is the "power of the keys", and also the power of double-edged weapons, which relates to the two snakes coiled in a spiral around the caduceus. — Guénon 1946

So we are looking at three centres which, despite different traditional interpretations, involve the same function. They fix on the sacred geography of India the three corners of Kāmarūpa/Traipurā, that same triangle which, in a microcosmic perspective, encloses in the *mūlādhāracakra* the energy of the Goddess, *kuṇḍalinī,* in her latent condition. In this way Assam which, significantly, lies at the far eastern reaches of India, functions as a boundary, a gateway leading in and out of the manifest world or — according to an equivalent temporal symbology — as the beginning and end of a cycle, thereby justifying the retraction of the Supreme Centre into this primordial land in the final phase of the Kali-Yuga.[3]

If we now go back to Guénon's observation and attempt to define whether the cult of the Yoginīs belongs to the Tantric path of the right hand (Dakṣiṇācāra) or the left hand (Vāmācāra), we realize immediately that it eludes this classification and, although it uses elements from both paths, rises to a quite different intellectual order.

This polarization, in fact, seems to pertain more to the sphere — which has so frequently emerged in the course of this study — of contradistinction between the cold/peaceful manifestations of the Goddess, which find expression in Vārāhī, Śītalā, Lalitākāntā, Mariyāmman and Ḍākinī, the handmaidens of Chinnamastā, and her hot-irate forms interpreted by Cāmuṇḍā, Mātaṅgī, Ugra-Tārā, Manasā, Yellammā, Śmaśāna Kāmākhyā and the handmaiden Varṇinī. A polarization reflected in Vajrayāna practice in the forms of sacred geography used in supports for meditation: rolling hills and flowering meadows favour the visualization of peaceful deities, whereas rugged cliffs, dark

[3] In this presentation of the three *nāḍīs* as rivers, along with the relation of Gaṅgā and Yamunā to *iḍā* and *piṅgalā*, the central *nāḍī*, the subtle or hidden one, is transposed from the vanished River Sarasvatī to the Tsangpo/Brahmaputra River system which emerges from the body of Dorje Pagmo.

rocks and sharp peaks tend to evoke irate gods.

Now, since Śāktism presents itself as a complete doctrinal system, it cannot be lacking in a more elevated view, that view which traditionally corresponds to identification with the supreme *Brahman* or to the Great Mysteries.

Therefore the Yoginīs — who preside over *śrīyantra* and the different *cakra*s of the human body, who pass beyond death, who dispense *siddhi* and knowledge, who constitute the "heart" of Śrīvidyā — are the ones who in the half-light outline all the elements of a Middle Way which is the heritage of the Śākta tradition in its highest form. The scarcity of external evidence for this Way, far from representing a limitation, suggests an extremely restricted and qualified *paramparā* capable of keeping under control a transmission which otherwise — due to the Tantric sphere on which it rests — might end up giving preference to the means rather than the end.

It is to this Middle Way, then, that other aspects of Devī allude — aspects like Tripurāsundarī, Kamākhyā, Chinnamastā, Reṇukā and Vajrayoginī-Vajravārāhī, who are all connected — not by chance — to the three traditional centres (*tīrtha*s) of Assam. In Vajrayāna sacred geography this correspondence is reflected in the waterfall, which evokes transitoriness, or at the microcosmic level, in the descent of *amṛta-soma* as a glandular secretion which diffuses from the cranial vault through all the *cakra*s.

For that matter, hints of a Way which can transcend the polarity of the manifest world are scattered throughout the entire Hindu tradition. According to *Bhagavad-Gītā*, in fact,

> [. . .] there are two *puruṣa*s, one perishable (*jīvātman*), the other indestructible (*ātman*): the first is divided up among all beings, the second is immutable. But there is another *puruṣa*, the highest (*uttama*), which is called *paramātman* and which, as the Everlasting Lord, penetrates and sustains the

> three worlds. Because I am beyond destructibility and even indestructibility (as the Supreme Principle of one and the other), I am celebrated in the world and in the Veda with the name of *Puruṣottama*.[4]

But Tripurasundarī — also called Śrīvidyā — is precisely she who "penetrates and sustains the three worlds", so that the other two *nāḍī*s, the other two *puruṣa*s, find in this text a direct correspondence with the time and the immutable knowledge represented by the Vedas, and with the knowledge divided among all beings, hence the individual knowledge represented by Tantric teachings.

It is this subtle level which identifies the entire parabola of the Yoginīs, passing through the constant of Devī-Knowledge-devouring Time and reiterating how in this period of *manvantara*, due to successive degenerations, Tantrism constitutes the only effective instrument for clearing and restoring the path towards knowledge, making possible a reintegration with the Absolute.[5]

This stance is echoed in numerous symbolic references, beginning with the wine and meat offered in the ritual libations which have replaced, almost universally, the blood of sacrifice. But wine is also an inferior surrogate for *soma*, the central element of Vedic sacrifice in another epoch, before the secret was lost and it became precluded to this human race. So it indicates the knowledge which can be obtained through the Tantric path, the only access to the "elixir of immortality" which is still possible in this last decadent phase of the Kali-Yuga. The same symbolism is hidden in the *pāśa*, the noose held in the Goddess's hand, signifying possession and sacrifice — sacrifice which suggests a chance for the victim to make contact with the higher states of being.

The flight of Yoginī-Ḍākinī reflected in her proximity to birds

---

4 *Bhagavad-Gītā*, XV.16-18, tr. Guénon 1925.

5 Guénon 1967.

of prey also evokes Garuḍa, the king of eagles, whose calling it is to perform the function of a psychopomp in accompanying beings towards liberation (*mokṣa*). And that same flight indicates the understanding of secret things and metaphysical truths because, as is set forth in *Pañcaviṁśa Brāhmaṇa*, "those who understand have wings".[6]

Again, note the command exercised by Manasā and Śītalā over snakes, whose poison is a cipher for transformation. Poison and transformation are echoed at a subtle level in the power of the serpent to reawaken *kuṇḍalinī-śakti*, the energy slumbering in every one of us, to make it rise along the *merudaṇḍa* passing through the succession of diverse Cakras–Yoginīs, finally arriving at the reintegration of the Perfect Man (*satpuruṣa*) and the reabsorption of individual manifestation.

Or again, the inclination towards sacrifice which is constantly evoked by the Yoginīs and is epitomized by replacement of the head of Reṇukā — hence the *pravargya-vidyā* — a synonym for initiatory death, a teaching which leads to *madhu-vidyā*, giving access to the supreme knowledge.

And it is in this setting that we should see the Yoginī who preside over the various points of *śrīyantra*, granting *siddhi* to practitioners not so much in the form of gross powers as — once again — of subtle knowledge, the cosmic potency of the Mahāvidyās capable of leading them out of the illusory world of *māyā*.

So possession, opening oneself to the kiss of the Goddess or her contagion, the voluptuous dance of skeletons, *eros* and *thanatos*, the experience of initiatory death — these are none other than the power of *vajra*, identification with the One through the

---

6 Eliade 1954. Furthermore *Gāyatrī* — the *mantra* which is given during the rite of Upanayana — is called the eagle which carries *soma* or, in a different version of the myth, transforms itself into a falcon to bring *soma* from the heavens.

annulment of opposites, dissolution and reabsorption into the sacred monosyllable *oṁ* inside the *ājñā cakra*, the two-petalled *cakra* which is the eye of knowledge.

And finally one reaches Kāmakalā, the supreme triangle and dwelling place of Śakti, root of all *mantras*, which ideally concludes the reabsorption of the Self which began with the reawakening of *kuṇḍalinī* at the base of *merudaṇḍa*, in the Traipurā triangle whose name is Kāmarūpa, the same name which on the sacred ground of Bhārata designates Assam. Beyond this there is only the doorway of *sahasrāra*, the thousand-petalled lotus which, like the wheel fixed to the top of the *yūpa*, allows the *cakravartin* — the Perfect Man — to leave the heaven of the fixed stars and rise to *satyaloka* (the heaven of truth) over which Paramaśiva presides.

Here all sequentiality is transmuted into simultaneity and all things remain in an eternal present, so that the apparent death evoked by the Yoginīs proves in reality to be a transformation into Transcendent Man, an identification of the supreme Self, (*paramātman*), from which *mokṣa* immediately results.

So the subtle door in that last corner of India, in the outermost heaven of the Kali-Yuga, comprehends the diluvial cycle which from the liberation of the celestial waters (Indra-Vr̥tra) through the precipitation of the Brahmaputra/Tsangpo on to the land of men, leads to the deluge of fire which will bring it to an end. But that door is above all the cosmic potency of Devī, a power which embodies Ultimate Knowledge, the identity between the knower, knowing and what is known.

Here Śrīvidyā takes the form of Kamalā, the antidote to the black night of Dhūmāvatī, the Mahāvidyā who dresses in water like a lotus flower, she who arose like Matsya at the beginning of time from the churning of the sea of milk. Or, from an equivalent viewpoint, she is Tripurasundarī, the Mahāvidyā who corresponds to Kalkin, the end of the cycle, she who through knowledge leads to the threshold of the supreme lotus.

Thus the darkness which cloaks the Yoginīs is *amāvasyā*, (black night), the night of cosmic dissolution and annihilation, the night which pervades the universe in the interstices between cycles of time. In this night where everything is lost, in this nothingness which separates the universes like the emptiness between one breath of Brahmā and the next, between one bead and the next of the *mālā*, the rosary which counts out the worlds, the Yoginīs extend their fearsome dominion, drinking toasts from *kapāla* and offering the fruits of sacrifice as a libation.

Yet this is the same darkness of the eclipse, the shining darkness guarded in the cavern of the heart. So *amāvasyā* turns out to be the reflection of the sixteenth Nityā, the image of Lalitā-Tripurasundarī herself.

This is the leap we must be capable of making, this is the tiger to be mounted, this is the *mantra śabara*, the wild *mantra* to which Svāmī Karapātrī alludes. That same Karapātrī who; in the first half of the last century, established alongside the metaphysical peaks and the purity of the Advaita Vedānta the retrieval of the teachings of *śrīvidyā*.

So the Yoginīs who today, nearly five centuries after the last temples were erected in their honour, have reappeared on the walls of the Tripurasundarī Mandira at Paramahaṁsī, seem to incarnate the *dvārapāla*s, the guards at the threshold of the Devī. Beyond them one can make out traces of the Middle Way, a subtle route where Śrīvidyā takes on the inebriation of the Absolute, embracing the beginning and the end, annihilation and liberation, and points out — in this final spurt of the Kali-Yuga — the *tīrtha* which leads through the horror of death to the recognition of *jīvātman* in the supreme *Brahman*.

So what is the nature of the Yoginīs? Have we perhaps ripped away their veils? Obviously not. And it could hardly be otherwise, or something else would necessarily have to emerge to take their place — to preside over that half light which comes between forces and powers lying dormant in the earth and the capacity to use them as a vehicle to transcendence; to bridge the gulf between tribal coarseness, the brutality of sacrifice, and possession by spirits on the one side and on the other, the ultimate secret, accessible through the path of initiation and the blade of metaphysics.

Hence the Yoginīs evoke the powers and the pitfalls of Tantra, cloaking themselves in an ambiguity which is entirely human, an echo of our imperfect comprehension which stubbornly clings to the perennial glitter of *māyā*. And yet, in all the evanescence of their function, they constitute a sign, a precise trace indicating the presence of a hidden opening, a way out of the always shimmering screen of the cosmos.

Bibliography

Arnoldo, L., 2002, "La dea che uccide il bufalo", in *Il sangue purificatore nel sacrificio del bufalo nell'Asia meridionale*, ed. A. Amadi, Venezia: AVIS.

Avalon, A., 1913, *Hymns to the Goddess*, Madras: Ganesh & Co.

———, 1919, *The Serpent Power*, London: Luzak & Co.

Baker, I., 2004, *The Heart of the World*, New York: Penguin.

Beggiora, S., 2003, *Sonum, spiriti della giungla. Lo sciamanismo delle tribù Saora dell'Orissa*, Milano: Franco Angeli.

———, 2009, "Spiriti delle acque e Dee della Mahānadi", in *I fiumi sacri - Indoasiatica* 6, ed. G.G. Filippi, Venezia: Cafoscarina.

Bhairavan, A., 2002, *Kālī's Oḍiyya: A Shaman's True Story of Initiation*, Varanasi: Pilgrims Publishing.

Bianchi, E., 2006, "Yamāntaka: il vincitore della morte nel buddhismo tantrico cinese e tibetano", in *L'ira degli Dei - Indoasiatica* 4, ed. M. Marchetto, Venezia: Cafoscarina.

Brooks, D.R., 1990, *The Secret of the Three Cities*, Chicago: University of Chicago Press.

———, 1992, *Auspicious Wisdom*, Albany: State University of New York Press.

Chalier, Visuvalingam E., 1986, "Bhairava: Kotwāl of Varanasi," in T.P. Verma (ed.) *Varanasi Through the Ages*, Varanasi: Bharatiya Itihas Sankalan Samiti, 1986.

Chatterjee, S.K., 1999, *Daśa Mahāvidyās*, Lucknow: Sri Soumitra Goswami Printers.

Coomaraswamy, A.K, 1924, *The Dance of Śiva: Essays on Indian Art and Culture*, New York: Sunwise Turn.

———, 1944, *Sir Gawain and the Green Knight: Indra and Namuci, Speculum* 19(1): 104-125.

———, 1977 "Ātmayajña: Self-Sacrifice", in R. Lipsey (ed.) *Coomaraswamy 2: Selected Papers. Metaphysics*, Princeton: Princeton University Press, Bollingen Series LXXXIX.

———, 1978, *La doctrine du sacrifice*, ed. G. Leconte, Paris: Dervy Livres.

———, 1980, *Yaksas*, New Delhi: Munshiram Manoharlal.

Crooke, W., 1978, *The Popular Religion and Folklore of Northern India*, 4th edn., 2 vols., New Delhi: Munshiram Manoharlal (1st edn., Mirzapur, 1893).

Daniélou, A., 1964, *Hindu Polytheism*, New York: Bollingen Foundation.

———, 1994, *L'erotismedivinisé*, Paris: Jacques Cloarec.

Dehejia, V., 1986, *Yoginī Cult and Temples: A Tantric Tradition*, New Delhi: National Museum.

Doniger O'Flaherty, W., 1975, *Hindu Myths: A Sourcebook Translated from the Sanskrit*, Harmondsworth: Penguin Classics.

———, 1976, *The Origins of Evil in Hindu Mythology*, Berkeley: University of California.

Durkheim, E. and M. Mauss, 2002, *De quelquesformes de classification — contribution à l'étude des représentations collectives*, Annéesociologique — vol. 6, 1901-02, Paris: Les Presses universitaires de France.

Eliade, M., 1951, *Le Chamanisme et les techniques archaïques de l'extase*, Paris: Payot.

———, 1954, *Le Yoga, immortalité et liberté*, Paris: Payot.

Ferrari, F., 2006, "Śitalā e le Madri ambigue del Bengala", in *L'ira degli Dei — Indoasiatica* 4, ed. M. Marchetto, Venezia: Cafoscarina.

Filippi, G.G., 1978a, "Kīrttimukha e Kālamukha", in *Annali di Ca' Foscari*, XVII (3), Venezia.

———, 1978b, *Post mortem et libération d'après Shankaracharya*, Quaderni dell'Unicorno, Milano: Archè.

———, 1978c, *Tantrismo e Arte*, Quaderni dell'Unicorno, Milano: Archè.

———, 1980, "The Celestial Ride", in R. Mastromattei and Rigopoulos *Shamanic Cosmos: From India to the North Pole Star*, Venetian Academy of Indian Studies Series 1, New Delhi: D.K. Printworld.

———, 1993, "On Some Sacrificial Features of the Mahiṣamardinī", in *Annali di Ca' Foscari*, XXXII(3).

———1995, "On Some Aspects of Bhūtas in the Birth–Death Passages", in B.N. Saraswati (ed.), *Prakṛti: The Integral Vision*, New Delhi: D.K. Printworld.

———, 1996, "La dolcezza del sapere: Madhu Vidyā", in A. Cadonna (ed.) *Ricordo di Alain Daniélou*, Firenze: Leo Olschki Editore.

———, 1999, *Mṛtyu: Concept of Death in Indian Traditions*, New Delhi: D.K. Printworld.

———, 2002, "Il movimento della Devī: un'epidemia di possessione collettiva", in *Annali di Ca' Foscari* - anno XLI, Venezia.

———, 2006, "Conservazione delle ceneri umane nell'India tradizionale. La dottrina del resto", in F. Remotti (ed.) *Morte e trasformazione dei corpi. Interventi di tanatometamorfosi*, Milano: Paravia Bruno Mondadori.

———, 2008, "L'incompiuto di Mamallapuram", *L. Omacini L'opera incompiuta, Annali di Ca' Foscari*, XLVII, 2, Padova.

———, 2008, "Oracles and Shamans in Arunachal Pradesh", *Central Asiatic Journal*, 52(1).

Flood, G.D., 1996, *An Introduction to Hinduism*, Cambridge: Cambridge University Press.

Gait, E.A., 1906, *A History of Assam*, Calcutta: Thacker, Spink & Co.

Goswamy, K.P., 1998, *Kāmākhyā Temple*, New Delhi: A.P.H. Publishing House.

Griffith, Ralph T.H., 1987, *Hymns of the Rgveda*, Delhi: Munshiram Manoharlal.

Grunwedel, A., 1915, "Der Wegnach Shambhala", *Abhandlung der Konoglich Bayerischen Akademie der Wissenschaften*, 29(3).

Guénon, R., 1921 , *Introduction générale à l'étude des doctrines hindoues*, Paris: Marcel Rivière.

———, 1925, *L'Homme et son devenir selon le Vedānta*, Paris: Bossard.

———, 1946, *La grande triade*, Paris: Gallimard.

———, 1962, *Symboles fondamentaux de la Science sacrée*, Paris: Gallimard .

———, 1967, étudessurl'Hindouisme, Paris: Editions Traditionnelles.

Gyatso, K., 2000, *Guide to Ḍākinī Land*, Delhi: Motilal Banarsidass.

Hauer, J.W., 1922, *Die Anfänge der Yogapraxis in alten Indien*, Berlin: W. Kohlhammer.

Heesterman, J.C., 1993, *The Broken World of Sacrifice*, Chicago: The University of Chicago Press.

Hillebrandt, A., 1980, *Vedic Mythology*, 1st Indian edn., Delhi: Motilal Banarsidass (1st edn., Vedische Mythologie, Breslau, 1891).

Hubert, H. and M. Mauss, 1909, *Mélanges d'histoire des religions*, Paris: Alcan.

Karpatri (Svāmi), 2009, *The Liṅga and the Great Goddess*, Varanasi: Indica Books.

Kinsley, D., 1975, "Freedom from Death in the Worship of Kālī", *Numen*, XXII(III).

———, 1998, *Tantric Visions of the Divine Feminine*, Delhi: Motilal Banarsidass.

Kramrisch, S., 1981, *The Presence of Śiva*, New York: Princeton University Press.

Lévi, S., 1898, *La Docrine du sacrifice dans les Brāhmaṇa*, Paris: E. Leroux.

Mackenzie, Brown C., 1990, *The Triumph of the Goddess: The Canonical Models and Theological Visions of the Devī-Bhāgavata Purāṇa*, Albany: State University of New York Press.

Malamoud, C., 2002, *Le jumeausolaire*, Paris: Editions du Seuil.

———, 2005, *Féminité de la parole*, Paris: Albin Michel.

Marchetto, M., 2002, "Il sangue nella mitologia śākta", in A. Amadi (ed.) *Il sangue purificatore nel sacrificio del bufalo nell'Asia meridionale*, Venezia: AVIS.

Mastromattei, R., 1988, *La Terra Reale. Dèi, spiriti, uomini del Nepal*, Roma: V. Levi ed.

Mishra, N.R., 2004, *Kāmākhyā: A Socio-Cultural Study*, New Delhi: D.K. Printworld.

Misra, O.P., 1989, *Iconography of the Saptamātr̥kā*, New Delhi: Agam Kala Prakashan.

Mookerjee, A., 1982, *Kundalini: The Arousal of the Inner Energy*, London: Thames and Hudson.

Oldham, C.F., 1988, *The Sun and the Serpent*, New Delhi: Asian Educational Services.

Oppert, G., 1893, *On the Original Inhabitants of Bhāratavarṣa or India*, Westminster: Constable.

Panikkar, S.K., 1997, *Saptamātṛkā Worship and Sculptures*, New Delhi: D.K. Printworld.

Pelissero, A. (ed.), 1995, *Il segreto della Dea Tripurā*, Torino: Ananke.

Pellegrini, G., 2006, "Il mito della bhairavotpatti: una ricostruzione", in *L'ira degli Dei — Indoasiatica* 4, ed. M. Marchetto, Venezia: Cafoscarina.

———, (ed.), 2009, *L'uomo e il sacro in India: Svāmī Karapātrī, Indoasiatica* 5, Venezia: Cafoscarina.

P'u Sung-ling, 1913, *Strange Stories from the Lodge of Leisure*, London: Constable.

Purakayastha, S., 1992, "The Concept of Śakti in Early Assam", *Journal of the Assam Research Society*, XXXII(1-2).

Rakesh, V.D., 2004, *Daśamahāvidyā-Mīmāṁsā*, New Delhi: Sanjay Prakashan.

Ramasso, C., 2004, "Ekapādamūrti: dall'uno ai molti, Rudra e i Rudra", *Arte oltre le forme - Indoasiatica* 1, ed. G. Torcinovich, Venezia: Cafoscarina.

———, 2009, "La storia di Hemālekha nell'ottica dottrinale di Svāmī Karapātrī", in G. Pellegrini (ed.) *L'uomo e il sacro in India. Svāmī Karapātrī - Indoasiatica* 5, Venezia: Cafoscarina.

———, 2010, "Some Notes on the Kāmākhyā Pīṭha", in Rana P.B. Singh (ed.) *Sacred Geography of Goddesses in South Asia*, Newcastle upon Tyne: Cambridge Scholars Publishing.

Rao, S.K.Ramachandra, 1989, *Pratima Kosha*, Bangalore: Kalpatharu Research Academy.

———, 2005a, *Śrīvidyā-Kośa*, Delhi: Sri Satguru Publications.

———, 2005b, *The Tantrik Practices in Śrī-Vidyā*, Delhi: Sri Satguru Publications.

———, 2008, *Śrī-Chakra: Its Yantra, Mantra and Tantra*, Delhi: Sri Satguru Publications.

Rath, J., 2009, "The Concept of Mother Goddess in the Art and Literature of Orissa", *Orissa Review*, September.

Rigopoulos, A., 2000, *Dattātreya: The Immortal Guru, Yogi and Avatāra*, Delhi: Sri Satguru Publications.

Saletore, R.N., 1981, *Indian Witchcraft: A Study in Indian Occultism*, New Delhi: Abhinav Publications.

Santillana, G. (de) & Dechend H. (von), 1969, *Hamlet's Mill: An Essay on Myth and the Frame of Time*, Boston: Gambit.

Satpathy, S., 1991, *Śakti Iconography in Tantric Mahāvidyās*, Calcutta: P.K. Bhattacharya.

Schwarz, A., 2009, *La donna e l'amore al tempo dei miti*, Milano: Garzanti.

Sermonti, G., 2002, *Il mito della grande madre*, Milano: Mimesis.

Sharma, R.K., 1978, *The Temple of Chauṅsaṭha-Yoginī at Bheraghat*, New Delhi: Agam Kala Prakashan.

Singh, G.P., 1990, *Kirātas in Ancient India*, New Delhi: Gian Publishing House.

Torcinovich, G., 1980, "The Horse and the Journey to Heaven of the Shaman and the Vedic Sacrificer", in R. Mastromattei and A. Rigopoulos (eds.) *Shamanic Cosmos: From India to the North Pole Star*, Venetian Academy of Indian Studies Series 1, New Delhi: D.K. Printworld.

Venkateswara, S.V., 1928, *Indian Culture Through the Ages*, London: Longmans Green and Co.

White D.G., 1996, *The Alchemical Body*, Chicago: The University of Chicago Press.

———, 2003, *Kiss of the Yoginī: 'Tantric Sex' in Its South Asian Contexts*, Chicago: The University of Chicago Press.

Zanderigo, G., 2002, "Il bufalo nei riti funerari del sud-est asiatico", in A. Amadi (ed.) *Il sangue purificatore nel sacrificio del bufalo nell'Asia meridionale*,Venezia: AVIS.

———, 2009, "La discesa del Gange semplice rappresentazione di un mito?", in G.G. Filippi (ed.) *I fiumi sacri - Indoasiatica* 6, Venezia: Cafoscarina.

———, 2014, "Dal Kalkin all'estinzione dei mondi: dei molti inizi e delle molte fini", in S. Beggiora (ed.) *Pralaya. La fine dei tempi nelle tradizioni d'Oriente e d'Occidente – Quaderni di Indoasiatica*, Roma: Novalogos.

Zimmer, H., 1946, *Myths and Symbols in Indian Art and Civilization*, New York: Pantheon Books.

Zolla, E., 2002, *Discesa all'Ade e resurrezione*, Milano: Adelphi.

Visuals

fig. 1: Temple of the Cauṅsaṭha-Yoginī, Hirapur, Odisha, ninth-tenth century

fig. 2: Temple of the Cauṅsaṭha-Yoginī, Bherāghāṭ, Madhya Pradesh, tenth-eleventh century

fig. 3: Śrī Erūḍī Yoginī, temple of the Cauṅsaṭha-Yoginī, Bherāghāṭ
Madhya Pradesh, tenth-eleventh century

fig. 4a: Battle of the Aṣṭamātṛkā against the demon Raktabīja. Painting on paper from *Devī-Māhātmya* manuscript, Nepal, eighteenth century

fig. 4b: Durgā battling the demon Raktabīja while Kālī collects the blood with her tongue. Painting on paper, nineteenth century

fig. 5: Dhūmāvatī, painting on paper

fig. 6: Nirr̥ti, painting on paper

fig. 7: Cāmuṇḍā (Caṇḍikā), temple of the Cauṅsaṭha-Yoginīs, Bherāghāṭ Madhya Pradesh, tenth-eleventh century

fig. 8: Vārāhī, painting on paper

fig. 9: Patañjali, wood sculpture, Tamil Nadu, early twentieth century

fig. 10: Saptamātr̥kā, Airāvateśvara Temple
Darasuram, Tamil Nadu, twelfth century

fig. 11: Kālī, statue in painted clay, Guwahati, Assam

fig. 12: Yoginī Temple, Khajurāho, Madhya Pradesh, ninth-tenth century. A rare example of a temple dedicated to the Yoginīs having a rectangular plan

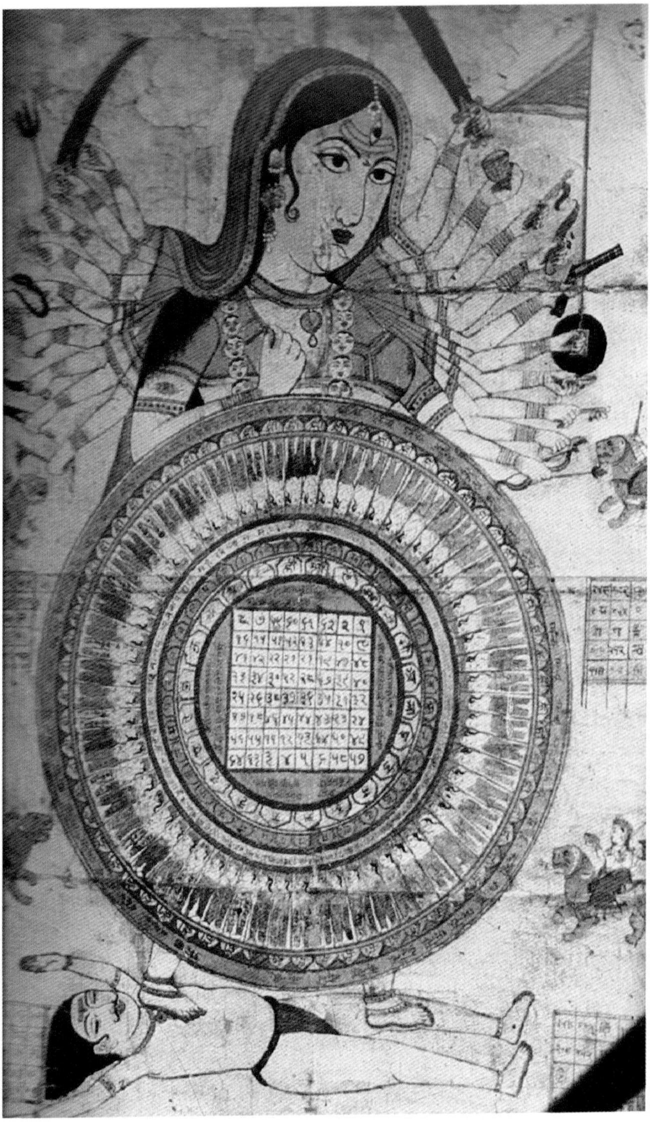

fig. 13: Devī with *yoginī cakra*, painting on cloth
Rajasthan, eighteenth-nineteenth century

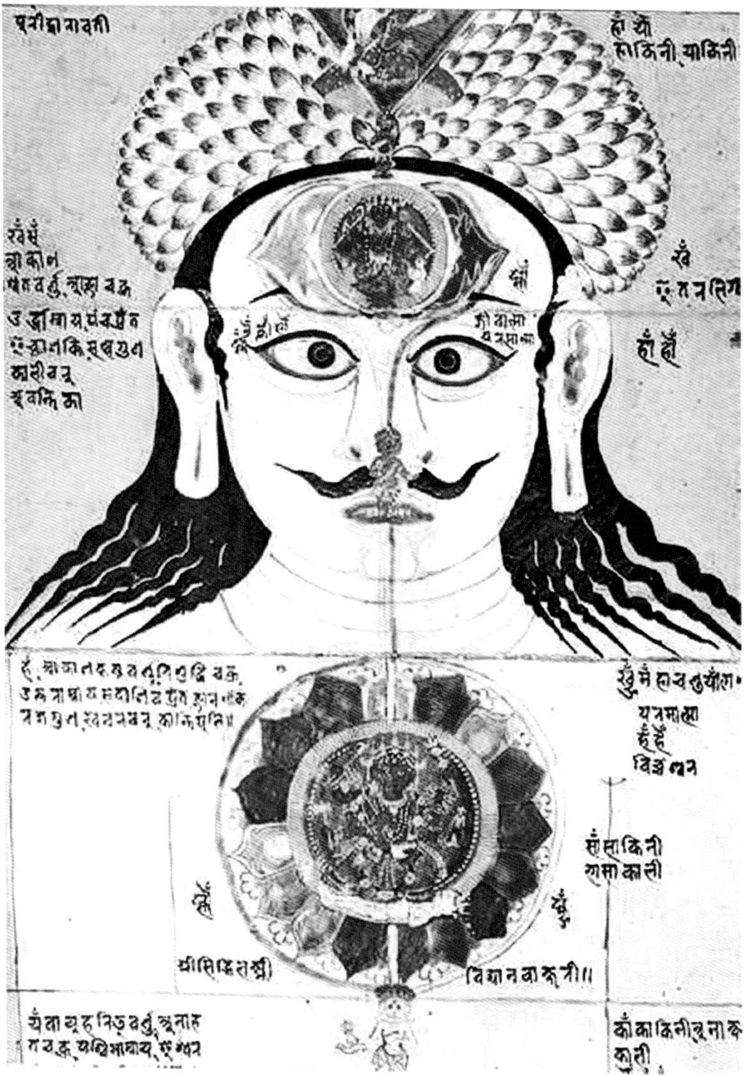

fig. 14: *Ājñā cakra*, painting on paper, Nepal, seventeenth century

fig. 15: *Śrīcakra* maṇḍala

fig. 16: Vajravārāhī Yantra Maṇḍala, painting on canvas
Tibet, nineteenth century

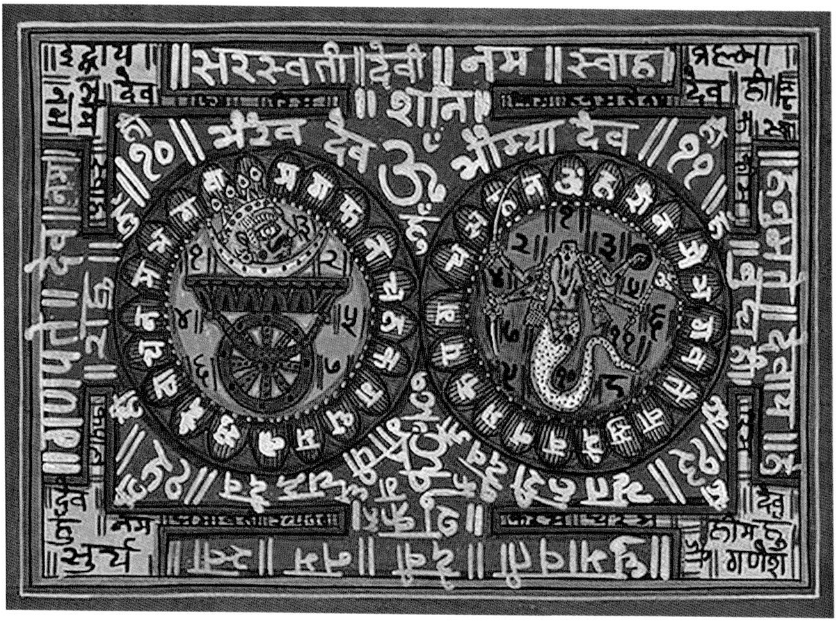

fig. 17: Rāhu and Ketu, painting on paper

fig. 18: Rāhu, wood panel, Tamil Nadu, nineteenth century

fig. 19: Ketu, cast bronze

fig. 20: Yantra of the sixteen Nityā

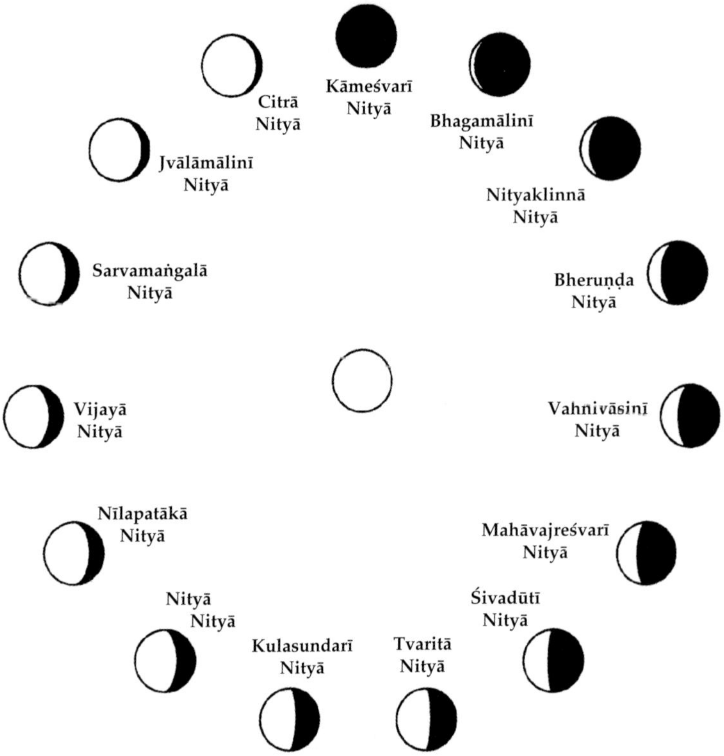

fig. 21: Representation of the sixteen Nityās (lunar kalās)

fig. 22: Yakṣiṇī, terracotta, Śuṅga dynasty, second-first century BCE

fig. 23: World tree/axis mundi. Its image is symbolically inverted so that its roots sink into the sky

fig. 24: Sculptures of *nāgakāla* at the foot of a *kulavṛkṣa* tree
Brahmadesan, Tamil Nadu

fig. 25: Yoginī seated on a tiger skin, Mughal miniature

fig. 26: Durgā Mahiṣāsuramardinī. Low relief from the Pallava period, cave of Mahiṣamardinī, Mahabalipuram, Tamil Nadu, seventh century

fig. 27: Bhairavī with a *yogin* in a cremation ground

fig. 28: *Yoginī*

fig. 29: Śītalā Devī

fig. 30: Manasā Devī

fig. 31: Paraśurāma beheads his mother Reṇukā, obeying the order of his father Jamadagni

fig. 32: Mātaṅgī Devī

fig. 33: Māyārūpa Yellammā

fig. 34: Ekavīra, temple of Saṅkaṭa-Mocana, Varanasi, Uttar Pradesh

fig. 35: Mātṛ-Rūpā, Lajjā-Gaurī Devī, from the temple of Nāganātha, Nāganāthakolla, Bijapur district, Karnataka

fig. 36: Chinnamastā with Jayā and Vijayā

fig. 37: Beheading of the demon Mahiṣāsura, from whose neck emerges the *liṅga*

fig. 38: Chinnamuṇḍā, Tangka, Tibet, mid-twentieth century

fig. 39: Śiva carrying the lifeless body of Satī, painting on paper, Kāṅgṛā, Himachal Pradesh, eighteenth century

fig. 40: Kālī dancing on a corpse, miniature, Kāṅgṛā, Himachal Pradesh, 1800-1825

fig. 41: Temple of Kāmākhyā, Gauhati, Assam

fig. 42: Kāmākhyā Devī

fig. 43: Śmaśāna Kālī

fig. 44: Dorje Pagmo (Vajravārāhī). Note the boar's head emerging from one side of the Goddess's head

fig. 45: Vasiṣṭha-Kuṇḍa, Gauhati, Assam

fig. 46: Paraśurāma-Kuṇḍa, Arunachal Pradesh

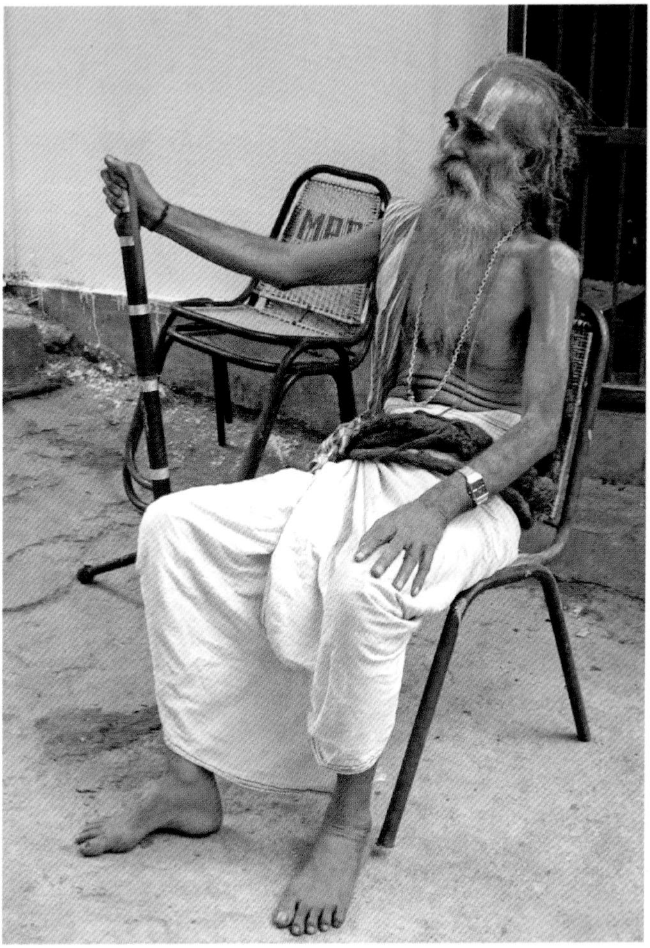

fig. 47: Hari Bābā, Paraśurāma-Kuṇḍa, Arunachal Pradesh

fig. 48: Paraśurāma-Kuṇḍa, Arunachal Pradesh,
the cave where according to tradition, Paraśurāma hid

fig. 49: Temple of Aśvakrānta, seventeenth century, Gauhati, Assam

fig. 50: Tīrtha of Aśvakrānta, north bank of the Brahmaputra near Gauhati, Assam

fig. 51: Kṛṣṇa battling the demon Narakāsura, painting on paper
Delhi–Agra, mid-sixteenth century

fig. 52: Aśvamedha, painting on paper

fig. 53: Kalkin, wall painting, Tamil Nadu, in this example Kalkin, like Hayagrīva, is respresented with a horse's head

fig. 54: Hayagrīva (Viṣṇu Vājimukha), Sambor Prei Kuk
Cambodia, tenth century

fig. 55: Aśvins, solar twins

fig. 56: *Yantra* of the *yoni*. In the centre it is possible to see the tripartite division of the central point (*bindu*)

fig. 57: *Yantra* of Vajrayoginī, made up of two overlapping triangles, Tibetan *maṇḍala* painting, nineteenth century

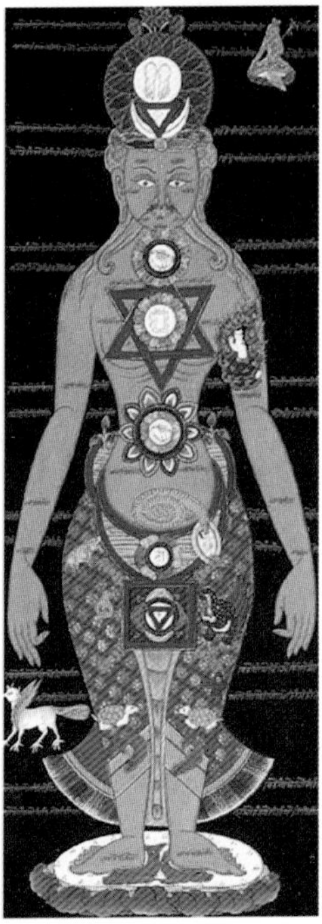

fig. 58: Image of the human body with its *cakra*s

fig. 59: Lalitā Tripurasundarī Devī

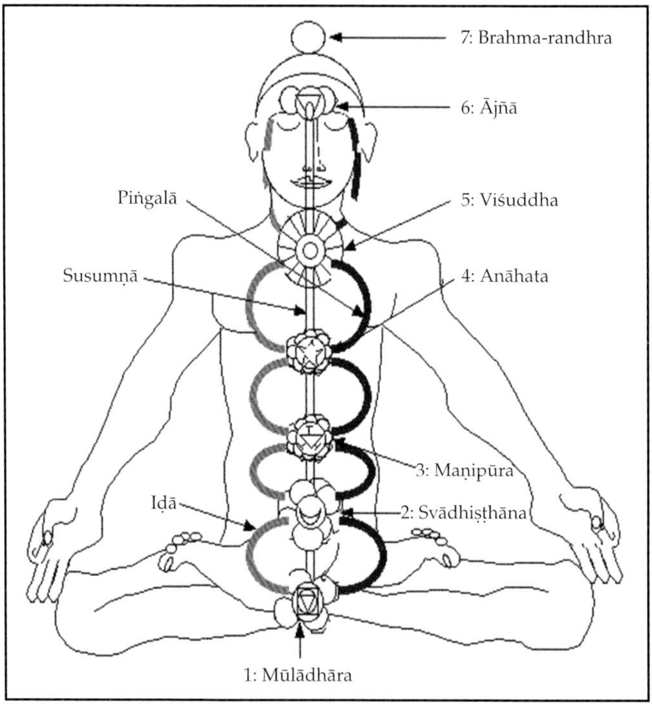

fig. 60: Image of the human body with the three *nāḍīs*

fig. 61: Dorje ritual instrument

Index

[Numbers in **normal type** indicate the pages with references in the body of the text. Numbers in **italics** indicate the pages with references in the footnotes. Numbers in **heavy type** refer to colour plates.]